# ABOUT THIS WOR

This workbook was designed to facilitate English Language Learners (ELLs) in their language development. The importance of practice and application is the foundation for this resource. It is important that English Language Learners are given the guidance, support, and opportunities to practice language learning in familiar and academic context.

The workbook activities coincide with the California English Language Development Standards. Educators can track and record their students' progression and acquisition of the English language.

Guided activities provide both educators and ELLs with appropriate levels of support. The activities expose the students to the format and language expectations of the English Language Proficiency Assessment for California (ELPAC). Similar to a test prep manual, this workbook will help familiarize ELLs with the ELPAC. However, this workbook can be a great resource to ALL language learners and doesn't have to be limited to just EL students.

The practice activities are another added layer of support for ELLs. The expected outcome of English language acquisition can be complemented with this great resource!

# OTHER ELPAC RESOURCES AVAILABLE:

### KINDERGARTEN
SPEAKING

LISTENING

READING

WRITING


### FIRST GRADE
SPEAKING

LISTENING

READING

WRITING


### SECOND GRADE
SPEAKING

LISTENING

READING

WRITING


### THIRD-FIFTH GRADE
LISTENING

READING

WRITING

# Table of Contents

## Speaking

# Talk About a Scene

# Speech Functions

# Support an Opinion

# Retell a Narrative

# Summarize an Academic Presentation

# Speaking
## *Talk About a Scene*

**This section includes:**
- Guided Activities
- Teacher's ELD Standards Record Sheet
- Student Practice Activities:
  - Constructive Conversations Guide
  - Talk About a Scene Student Practice

- - - - - - - - - - - - - - - - - - - - - - - - - - - - - - - - - - -

| **Alignment to CA ELD Standards:** | **Alignment to CCSS:** |
| --- | --- |
| **Part I: Interacting in Meaningful Ways** | |
| A.1 Exchanging Information & Ideas | SL.3.1, 6; L.3.1, 3, 6 |
| Exchanging information and ideas with others | SL.4.1, 6; L.4.1, 3, 6 |
| through oral collaborative conversations on a range | SL.5.1, 6; L.5.1, 3, 6 |
| of social and academic topics | |
| **Part II: Learning About How English Works** | W.3.5; SL.3.6; L.3.1, 3, 6 |
| B.3 Expanding & Enriching Ideas | W.4.5; SL.4.6; L.4.1, 3, 6 |
| Using verbs and verb phrases | W.5.5; SL.5.6; L.5.1, 3, 6 |
| **Part II: Learning About How English Works** | W.3.5; SL.3.6; L.3.1, 3, 6 |
| B.4 Expanding & Enriching Ideas | W.4.5; SL.4.6; L.4.1, 3, 6 |
| Using nouns and noun phrases | W.5.5; SL.5.6; L.5.1, 3, 6 |
| **Part II: Learning About How English Works** | W.3.5; SL.3.4, 6; L.3.1, 3, 6 |
| B.5 Expanding & Enriching Ideas | W.4.5; SL.4.4, 6; L.4.1, 3, 6 |
| Modifying to add details | W.5.5; SL.5.4, 6; L.5.1, 3, 6 |

- - - - - - - - - - - - - - - - - - - - - - - - - - - - - - - - - - -

**Guided Activities Direction:**
1. Show students the picture.
2. Follow the teacher directions.
3. **Say** the **Teacher Script** (indicated by  )
4. Guide students through:
   - Responding in English with words, short phrases, or a longer response
5. Then have students practice with additional speaking activities.

# Guided Activity #1

 **SAY** Show the student the picture.

**Look at the picture.
I am going to ask you some
questions about it.**

 **SAY** 1

**What is the boy in the back
doing?**

 **SAY** 2

**What is on the floor?**

 **SAY** 3

**Where do you think this is?**
After student responds, ask the follow-up question.
**How do you know?**

 **SAY** 4

**Describe what the girl is doing.**

 **SAY** 5

**Describe what the teacher is doing.**

 **SAY** 6

Point to the entire picture.
**Tell me something else about the picture.**

# Guided Activity #1

# Guided Activity #2

• • • • • • • • • • • • • • • • • • • • • • • • • • • • • • • • • • • • • • • •

 Show the student the picture.

**Look at the picture.
I am going to ask you some questions about it.**

 **1**

**What are the kids at the table doing?**

 **2**

**What is the lady doing?**

 **3**

**Where do you think this is?**
After student responds, ask the follow-up question.
**How do you know?**

 **4**

**Describe what the boy with the hat is doing.**

 **5**

**Describe what is on the wall.**

 **6**

Point to the entire picture.
**Tell me something else about the picture.**

# Guided Activity #2

## Speaking: *Talk About a Scene*

# Guided Activity #3

 **SAY** Show the student the picture.

**Look at the picture.
I am going to ask you some
questions about it.**

 **SAY** **1**

**What is the boy doing?**

 **SAY** **2**

**What is the girl?**

 **SAY** **3**

**Where do you think this is?**
After student responds, ask the follow-up question.
**How do you know?**

 **SAY** **4**

**Describe what the teacher is doing.**

 **SAY** **5**

**Describe what is on the building.**

 **SAY** **6**

Point to the entire picture.
**Tell me something else about the picture.**

# Guided Activity #3

# Guided Activity #4

 **SAY** Show the student the picture.
**Look at the picture.
I am going to ask you some
questions about it.**

 **SAY** **1**

**What is the teacher doing?**

 **SAY** **2**

**What is on the table?**

 **SAY** **3**

**Where do you think this is?**
After student responds, ask the follow-up question.
**How do you know?**

 **SAY** **4**

**Describe what the boy is doing.**

 **SAY** **5**

**Describe what the girl is doing.**

 **SAY** **6**

Point to the entire picture.
**Tell me something else about the picture.**

# Guided Activity #4

# Guided Activity #5

 Show the student the picture.

**Look at the picture.
I am going to ask you some
questions about it.**

 **1**

**What is the girl doing?**

**2**

**What is the teacher doing?**

 **3**

**Where do you think this is?**
After student responds, ask the follow-up question.
**How do you know?**

 **4**

**Describe what the kid in the back is doing.**

 **5**

**Describe what is on the stage.**

 **6**

Point to the entire picture.
**Tell me something else about the picture.**

# Guided Activity #5

**Speaking:** *Talk About a Scene*

# ELD Standards Record Sheet

<u>Directions:</u>

1. Look at the CA ELD Standards (**BELOW**) that correspond to this section.
2. Reference these specific standards for the template Record Sheet.
3. Use the following template Record Sheet to monitor students' proficiency levels for the **GUIDED ACTIVITIES** in this section.
4. Fill out all the information.  Circle, check, highlight the proficiency level. (*There is space for 20 students.  Make additional copies, as needed*)
5. Retain for your records to be used during grading, parent/student conferences, lesson planning, ELD documentation, etc.

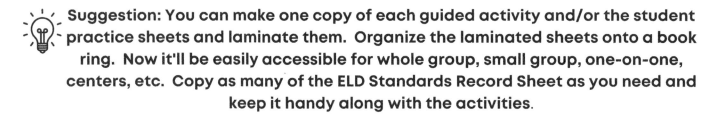 **Suggestion: You can make one copy of each guided activity and/or the student practice sheets and laminate them.  Organize the laminated sheets onto a book ring.  Now it'll be easily accessible for whole group, small group, one-on-one, centers, etc.  Copy as many of the ELD Standards Record Sheet as you need and keep it handy along with the activities**.

# ELD Standards Record Sheet

## CA ELD Standards & Proficiency Levels

**Part I:** Interacting in Meaningful Ways
*A.1 Exchanging Information & Ideas*

| EMERGING (EM) | EXPANDING (EX) | BRIDGING (BR) |
|---|---|---|
| Requires **Substantial** Support | Requires **Moderate** Support | Requires **Light** Support |
| **GRADE 3** | | |
| • Contribute to conversations & express ideas w/ basic conventions<br>• Ask/answer yes-no and wh-questions<br>• Respond using short phrases | • Contribute to *class, group, & partner discussions, including sustained dialogue by:*<br>• *Follows turn-taking rules*<br>• *Asking relevant questions*<br>• *Affirming others*<br>• *Adding relevant information* | • Contributes to*, initiates and sustains dialogue to class, group, & partner discussions by:*<br>• Follows turn-taking rules<br>• Asking relevant questions<br>• Affirming others<br>• Adding relevant information<br>• *Building on responses*<br>• *Providing useful feedback* |
| **GRADE 4** | | |
| • Contribute to conversations & express ideas w/ basic conventions<br>• Ask/answer yes-no and wh-questions<br>• Respond using short phrases | • Contribute to *class, group, & partner discussions, including sustained dialogue by:*<br>• *Follows turn-taking rules*<br>• *Asking relevant questions*<br>• *Affirming others*<br>• *Adding relevant information* | • Contributes to, *initiates and sustains dialogue* to class, group, & partner discussions by:<br>• Follows turn-taking rules<br>• Asking relevant questions<br>• Affirming others<br>• Adding relevant information<br>• *Building on responses*<br>• *Providing useful feedback* |
| **GRADE 5** | | |
| • Contribute to conversations & express ideas w/ basic conventions<br>• Ask/answer yes-no and wh-questions<br>• Respond using short phrases | • Contribute to *class, group, & partner discussions, including sustained dialogue by:*<br>• *Follows turn-taking rules*<br>• *Asking relevant questions*<br>• *Affirming others*<br>• *Adding relevant information* | • Contributes to, *initiates and sustains dialogue* to class, group, & partner discussions by:<br>• Follows turn-taking rules<br>• Asking relevant questions<br>• Affirming others<br>• Adding relevant information<br>• *Building on responses*<br>• *Providing useful feedback* |

# ELD Standards Record Sheet

## CA ELD Standards & Proficiency Levels

**Part II:** Learning About How English Works
### B.3 Using Verbs and Verb Phrases

| EMERGING (EM) | EXPANDING (EX) | BRIDGING (BR) |
|---|---|---|
| Requires **Substantial** Support | Requires **Moderate** Support | Requires **Light** Support |
| **GRADE 3** | | |
| • Use frequently used verbs<br>• Use different verb types (e.g. doing, saying, being/having, thinking/feeling)<br>• Use different verb tenses (e.g. simple past for recounting an experience)<br>• Appropriate for the text type and discipline to convey time | • Use a <u>growing number</u> of verb types (e.g. doing, saying, being/having, thinking/feeling)<br>• Use a <u>growing number</u> of verb tenses (e.g. simple past for retelling, simple present for a science description)<br>• Appropriate for the text type and discipline to convey time | • Use a <u>variety</u> of verb types (e.g. doing, saying, being/having, thinking/feeling)<br>• Use a <u>variety</u> of verb tenses (e.g. simple present for a science description, simple future to predict)<br>• Appropriate for the text type and discipline to convey time |
| **GRADE 4** | | |
| • Use various verbs<br>• Use various verb types (e.g. doing, saying, being/having, thinking/feeling)<br>• Use various verb tenses (e.g. simple past for recounting an experience)<br>• Appropriate for the text type and discipline for familiar topics | • Use various verbs<br>• Use various verb types (e.g. doing, saying, being/having, thinking/feeling)<br>• Use various verb tenses (e.g. simple past for retelling, timeless present for science explanation)<br>• Appropriate for the <u>task</u>, text type and discipline<br>• <u>For an increasing variety of familiar and new topics</u> | • Use various verb<br>• Use various verb types (e.g. doing, saying, being/having, thinking/feeling)<br>• Use various verb tenses(e.g. timeless present for science explanation, mixture of past and present for historical information report)<br>• Appropriate for the task and text type<br>• For a <u>variety</u> of familiar and new topics |
| **GRADE 5** | | |
| • Use frequently used verbs (e.g. take, like, eat)<br>• Use various verb types (e.g. doing, saying, being/having, thinking/feeling)<br>• Use various verb tenses (e.g. simple past for recounting an experience)<br>• Appropriate for the text type and discipline for familiar topics | • Use <u>various</u> verb types (e.g. doing, saying, being/having, thinking/feeling)<br>• Use various verb tenses (e.g. simple past for retelling, timeless present for science a description)<br>• Appropriate for the <u>task</u>, text type and discipline<br>• <u>For an increasing variety of topics</u> | • Use various verb types (e.g. doing, saying, being/having, thinking/feeling)<br>• Use various verb tenses (e.g. timeless present for science description, mixture of past and present for narrative or history explanation)<br>• Appropriate for the task and text type<br>• For a <u>variety</u> of topics |

# ELD Standards Record Sheet

## CA ELD Standards & Proficiency Levels

**Part II:** Learning About How English Works
### *B.4 Using Nouns and Noun Phrases*

| EMERGING (EM) ➤ | EXPANDING (EX) ➤ | BRIDGING (BR) ➤ |
|---|---|---|
| *Requires **Substantial** Support* | *Requires **Moderate** Support* | *Requires **Light** Support* |
| | **GRADE 3** | |
| • *Expand noun phrases in simple ways in order to enrich:*<br>　○ *The meaning of sentences*<br>　○ *Add details about ideas, people, things, etc. (e.g. adding an adjective to a noun)* | • *Expand noun phrases in a <u>growing number</u> of ways in order to enrich:*<br>　○ *The meaning of sentences*<br>　○ *Add details about ideas, people, things, etc. (e.g. adding comparative/superlative adjectives to nouns)* | • *Expand noun phrases in a <u>variety</u> of ways in order to enrich:*<br>　○ *The meaning of sentences and*<br>　○ *Add details about ideas, people, things, etc. (e.g. adding comparative/superlative adjectives to nouns, simple clause embedding)* |
| | **GRADE 4** | |
| • *Expand noun phrases in simple ways in order to enrich:*<br>　○ *The meaning of sentences*<br>　○ *Add details about ideas, people, things, etc. (e.g. adding an adjective)* | • *Expand noun phrases in a <u>variety</u> of ways in order to enrich:*<br>　○ *The meaning of sentences*<br>　○ *Add details about ideas, people, things, etc. (e.g. adding adjectives to noun phrases or simple clause embedding)* | • *Expand noun phrases in an <u>increasing variety</u> of ways in order to enrich:*<br>　○ *The meaning of sentences and*<br>　○ *Add details about ideas, people, things, etc. (e.g. adding general academic adjectives and adverbs to noun phrases or more complex clause embedding)* |
| | **GRADE 5** | |
| • *Expand noun phrases in simple ways in order to enrich:*<br>　○ *The meaning of sentences*<br>　○ *Add details about ideas, people, things, etc. (e.g. adding an adjective to a noun)* | • *Expand noun phrases in a <u>variety</u> of ways in order to enrich:*<br>　○ *The meaning of sentences*<br>　○ *Add details about ideas, people, things, etc. (e.g. adding comparative/superlative adjectives to noun phrases or simple clause embedding)* | • *Expand noun phrases in an <u>increasing variety</u> of ways in order to enrich:*<br>　○ *The meaning of sentences*<br>　○ *Add details about ideas, people, things, etc. (e.g. adding comparative/superlative and general academic adjectives to noun phrases or more complex clause embedding)* |

**Speaking:** *Talk About a Scene*

# ELD Standards Record Sheet

## CA ELD Standards & Proficiency Levels

**Part II:** Learning About How English Works
### B.5 Modifying to Add Details

| EMERGING (EM) → | EXPANDING (EX) → | BRIDGING (BR) → |
|---|---|---|
| Requires **Substantial** Support | Requires **Moderate** Support | Requires **Light** Support |
| **GRADE 3** | | |
| • Expand sentences with adverbials (e.g. adverbs, adverb phrases, prepositional phrases)<br>• Use these to provide details about a familiar activity or process (e.g. time, manner, place, cause) (e.g. They walked to the soccer field.) | • Expand sentences with adverbials (e.g. adverbs, adverb phrases, prepositional phrases)<br>• Use these to provide details about a familiar or <u>new activity</u> or process (e.g. time, manner, place, cause) (e.g. They worked quietly; They ran across the soccer field.) | • Expand sentences with adverbials (e.g. adverbs, adverb phrases, prepositional phrases)<br>• Use these to provide details about a <u>range</u> of familiar and new activities or processes. (e.g. time, manner, place, cause) (e.g. They worked quietly all night in their room.) |
| **GRADE 4** | | |
| • Expand sentences with familiar adverbials (e.g. basic prepositional phrases)<br>• Use these to provide details about a familiar activity or process (e.g. time, manner, place, cause) (e.g. They walked to the soccer field.) | • Expand sentences with a <u>growing variety</u> of adverbials (e.g. adverbs, prepositional phrases)<br>• Use these to provide details about a familiar or <u>new activity</u> or process (e.g. time, manner, place, cause) (e.g. They worked quietly; They ran across the soccer field.) | • Expand sentences with a <u>variety</u> of adverbials (e.g. adverbs, adverb phrases, prepositional phrases)<br>• Use these to provide details about a <u>variety</u> of familiar and new activities or processes.(e.g. time, manner, place, cause) (e.g. They worked quietly all night in their room.) |
| **GRADE 5** | | |
| • Expand and enrich sentences with adverbials (e.g. adverbs, adverb phrases, prepositional phrases)<br>• Use these to provide details about a familiar activity or process (e.g. time, manner, place, cause) | • Expand and enrich sentences with adverbials (e.g. adverbs, adverb phrases, prepositional phrases)<br>• Use these to provide details about a familiar or <u>new activity</u> or process (e.g. time, manner, place, cause) | • Expand and enrich sentences with adverbials (e.g. adverbs, adverb phrases, prepositional phrases)<br>• Use these to provide details about a <u>variety</u> of familiar and new activities or processes.(e.g. time, manner, place, cause) |

# ELD Standards Record Sheet

**Teacher:** _____  **Class:** _____

**Standards:** *PI.A.1*

**Guided Activities and Proficiency Levels:**

| Students: | #1 | #2 | #3 | #4 | #5 |
|---|---|---|---|---|---|
| _____ | EM / EX / BR | EM / EX / BR | EM / EX / BR | EM / EX / BR | EM / EX / BR |
| _____ | EM / EX / BR | EM / EX / BR | EM / EX / BR | EM / EX / BR | EM / EX / BR |
| _____ | EM / EX / BR | EM / EX / BR | EM / EX / BR | EM / EX / BR | EM / EX / BR |
| _____ | EM / EX / BR | EM / EX / BR | EM / EX / BR | EM / EX / BR | EM / EX / BR |
| _____ | EM / EX / BR | EM / EX / BR | EM / EX / BR | EM / EX / BR | EM / EX / BR |
| _____ | EM / EX / BR | EM / EX / BR | EM / EX / BR | EM / EX / BR | EM / EX / BR |
| _____ | EM / EX / BR | EM / EX / BR | EM / EX / BR | EM / EX / BR | EM / EX / BR |
| _____ | EM / EX / BR | EM / EX / BR | EM / EX / BR | EM / EX / BR | EM / EX / BR |
| _____ | EM / EX / BR | EM / EX / BR | EM / EX / BR | EM / EX / BR | EM / EX / BR |
| _____ | EM / EX / BR | EM / EX / BR | EM / EX / BR | EM / EX / BR | EM / EX / BR |
| _____ | EM / EX / BR | EM / EX / BR | EM / EX / BR | EM / EX / BR | EM / EX / BR |
| _____ | EM / EX / BR | EM / EX / BR | EM / EX / BR | EM / EX / BR | EM / EX / BR |
| _____ | EM / EX / BR | EM / EX / BR | EM / EX / BR | EM / EX / BR | EM / EX / BR |
| _____ | EM / EX / BR | EM / EX / BR | EM / EX / BR | EM / EX / BR | EM / EX / BR |
| _____ | EM / EX / BR | EM / EX / BR | EM / EX / BR | EM / EX / BR | EM / EX / BR |
| _____ | EM / EX / BR | EM / EX / BR | EM / EX / BR | EM / EX / BR | EM / EX / BR |
| _____ | EM / EX / BR | EM / EX / BR | EM / EX / BR | EM / EX / BR | EM / EX / BR |
| _____ | EM / EX / BR | EM / EX / BR | EM / EX / BR | EM / EX / BR | EM / EX / BR |
| _____ | EM / EX / BR | EM / EX / BR | EM / EX / BR | EM / EX / BR | EM / EX / BR |
| _____ | EM / EX / BR | EM / EX / BR | EM / EX / BR | EM / EX / BR | EM / EX / BR |

**Speaking:** *Talk About a Scene*

# ELD Standards Record Sheet

**Teacher:** _____ **Class:** _____

**Standards:** *PII.B.3*

**Guided Activities and Proficiency Levels:**

| Students: | #1 | #2 | #3 | #4 | #5 |
|---|---|---|---|---|---|
| | EM / EX / BR | EM / EX / BR | EM / EX / BR | EM / EX / BR | EM / EX / BR |
| | EM / EX / BR | EM / EX / BR | EM / EX / BR | EM / EX / BR | EM / EX / BR |
| | EM / EX / BR | EM / EX / BR | EM / EX / BR | EM / EX / BR | EM / EX / BR |
| | EM / EX / BR | EM / EX / BR | EM / EX / BR | EM / EX / BR | EM / EX / BR |
| | EM / EX / BR | EM / EX / BR | EM / EX / BR | EM / EX / BR | EM / EX / BR |
| | EM / EX / BR | EM / EX / BR | EM / EX / BR | EM / EX / BR | EM / EX / BR |
| | EM / EX / BR | EM / EX / BR | EM / EX / BR | EM / EX / BR | EM / EX / BR |
| | EM / EX / BR | EM / EX / BR | EM / EX / BR | EM / EX / BR | EM / EX / BR |
| | EM / EX / BR | EM / EX / BR | EM / EX / BR | EM / EX / BR | EM / EX / BR |
| | EM / EX / BR | EM / EX / BR | EM / EX / BR | EM / EX / BR | EM / EX / BR |
| | EM / EX / BR | EM / EX / BR | EM / EX / BR | EM / EX / BR | EM / EX / BR |
| | EM / EX / BR | EM / EX / BR | EM / EX / BR | EM / EX / BR | EM / EX / BR |
| | EM / EX / BR | EM / EX / BR | EM / EX / BR | EM / EX / BR | EM / EX / BR |
| | EM / EX / BR | EM / EX / BR | EM / EX / BR | EM / EX / BR | EM / EX / BR |
| | EM / EX / BR | EM / EX / BR | EM / EX / BR | EM / EX / BR | EM / EX / BR |
| | EM / EX / BR | EM / EX / BR | EM / EX / BR | EM / EX / BR | EM / EX / BR |
| | EM / EX / BR | EM / EX / BR | EM / EX / BR | EM / EX / BR | EM / EX / BR |
| | EM / EX / BR | EM / EX / BR | EM / EX / BR | EM / EX / BR | EM / EX / BR |
| | EM / EX / BR | EM / EX / BR | EM / EX / BR | EM / EX / BR | EM / EX / BR |
| | EM / EX / BR | EM / EX / BR | EM / EX / BR | EM / EX / BR | EM / EX / BR |

# ELD Standards Record Sheet

**Teacher:** _____ **Class:** _____

**Standards**: *PII.B.4*

**Guided Activities and Proficiency Levels:**

| Students: | #1 | #2 | #3 | #4 | #5 |
|---|---|---|---|---|---|
| | EM / EX / BR | EM / EX / BR | EM / EX / BR | EM / EX / BR | EM / EX / BR |
| | EM / EX / BR | EM / EX / BR | EM / EX / BR | EM / EX / BR | EM / EX / BR |
| | EM / EX / BR | EM / EX / BR | EM / EX / BR | EM / EX / BR | EM / EX / BR |
| | EM / EX / BR | EM / EX / BR | EM / EX / BR | EM / EX / BR | EM / EX / BR |
| | EM / EX / BR | EM / EX / BR | EM / EX / BR | EM / EX / BR | EM / EX / BR |
| | EM / EX / BR | EM / EX / BR | EM / EX / BR | EM / EX / BR | EM / EX / BR |
| | EM / EX / BR | EM / EX / BR | EM / EX / BR | EM / EX / BR | EM / EX / BR |
| | EM / EX / BR | EM / EX / BR | EM / EX / BR | EM / EX / BR | EM / EX / BR |
| | EM / EX / BR | EM / EX / BR | EM / EX / BR | EM / EX / BR | EM / EX / BR |
| | EM / EX / BR | EM / EX / BR | EM / EX / BR | EM / EX / BR | EM / EX / BR |
| | EM / EX / BR | EM / EX / BR | EM / EX / BR | EM / EX / BR | EM / EX / BR |
| | EM / EX / BR | EM / EX / BR | EM / EX / BR | EM / EX / BR | EM / EX / BR |
| | EM / EX / BR | EM / EX / BR | EM / EX / BR | EM / EX / BR | EM / EX / BR |
| | EM / EX / BR | EM / EX / BR | EM / EX / BR | EM / EX / BR | EM / EX / BR |
| | EM / EX / BR | EM / EX / BR | EM / EX / BR | EM / EX / BR | EM / EX / BR |
| | EM / EX / BR | EM / EX / BR | EM / EX / BR | EM / EX / BR | EM / EX / BR |
| | EM / EX / BR | EM / EX / BR | EM / EX / BR | EM / EX / BR | EM / EX / BR |
| | EM / EX / BR | EM / EX / BR | EM / EX / BR | EM / EX / BR | EM / EX / BR |
| | EM / EX / BR | EM / EX / BR | EM / EX / BR | EM / EX / BR | EM / EX / BR |
| | EM / EX / BR | EM / EX / BR | EM / EX / BR | EM / EX / BR | EM / EX / BR |

# ELD Standards Record Sheet

**Teacher:** _____ **Class:** _____

**Standards**: *PII.B.5*          **Guided Activities and Proficiency Levels:**

| Students: | #1 | #2 | #3 | #4 | #5 |
|---|---|---|---|---|---|
| | EM / EX / BR | EM / EX / BR | EM / EX / BR | EM / EX / BR | EM / EX / BR |
| | EM / EX / BR | EM / EX / BR | EM / EX / BR | EM / EX / BR | EM / EX / BR |
| | EM / EX / BR | EM / EX / BR | EM / EX / BR | EM / EX / BR | EM / EX / BR |
| | EM / EX / BR | EM / EX / BR | EM / EX / BR | EM / EX / BR | EM / EX / BR |
| | EM / EX / BR | EM / EX / BR | EM / EX / BR | EM / EX / BR | EM / EX / BR |
| | EM / EX / BR | EM / EX / BR | EM / EX / BR | EM / EX / BR | EM / EX / BR |
| | EM / EX / BR | EM / EX / BR | EM / EX / BR | EM / EX / BR | EM / EX / BR |
| | EM / EX / BR | EM / EX / BR | EM / EX / BR | EM / EX / BR | EM / EX / BR |
| | EM / EX / BR | EM / EX / BR | EM / EX / BR | EM / EX / BR | EM / EX / BR |
| | EM / EX / BR | EM / EX / BR | EM / EX / BR | EM / EX / BR | EM / EX / BR |
| | EM / EX / BR | EM / EX / BR | EM / EX / BR | EM / EX / BR | EM / EX / BR |
| | EM / EX / BR | EM / EX / BR | EM / EX / BR | EM / EX / BR | EM / EX / BR |
| | EM / EX / BR | EM / EX / BR | EM / EX / BR | EM / EX / BR | EM / EX / BR |
| | EM / EX / BR | EM / EX / BR | EM / EX / BR | EM / EX / BR | EM / EX / BR |
| | EM / EX / BR | EM / EX / BR | EM / EX / BR | EM / EX / BR | EM / EX / BR |
| | EM / EX / BR | EM / EX / BR | EM / EX / BR | EM / EX / BR | EM / EX / BR |
| | EM / EX / BR | EM / EX / BR | EM / EX / BR | EM / EX / BR | EM / EX / BR |
| | EM / EX / BR | EM / EX / BR | EM / EX / BR | EM / EX / BR | EM / EX / BR |
| | EM / EX / BR | EM / EX / BR | EM / EX / BR | EM / EX / BR | EM / EX / BR |

# Practice Activities

---

It is crucial to guide students in having **Constructive Conversations** utilizing skills and strategies that help them develop into productive thinkers and speakers.

- Help students **formulate** their ideas and thinking.
- Help students **explain and extend** their thinking so that it's clear and concise.
- Help students **support** their ideas and thinking with relevant support and information (i.e. from the picture).
- Help students **engage** in constructive dialogue with others through understanding, listening, and **consensus**.

---

**Practice Activities Direction:**

1. Students can work with partners, small group, or with an adult.

2. Students take turns using the Constructive Conversations script to help guide them through discussions about the scenes.

3. Students follow turn-taking protocols and use the Constructive Conversations script to build their oral language.

**Speaker #1**'s script is indicated by

**Speaker #2**'s script is indicated by **S2**

# Practice Activity #1

**Directions:** Practice having a constructive conversation about the picture:

☐ With a partner ☐ In a small group ☐ With an adult

**S1** Look at the picture.
Describe one thing that you see.

**S2** I see...........................
What do you see in the picture?

**S1** In the picture, I see........................
Can you describe something else in the picture?

**S2** I see...........................
What do you think?

**S1** I think.............
Where do you think this is and how do you know?

**S2** I think............
Do you agree or disagree?

**S1** I agree (disagree) because.............
Is there anything else you would like to add about the picture?

**S2** I would like to add...........

# Practice Activity #2

**Directions:** Practice having a constructive conversation about the picture:

☐ With a partner     ☐ In a small group     ☐ With an adult

**S1** Look at the picture.
Describe one thing that you see.

**S2** I see...........................
What do you see in the picture?

**S1** In the picture, I see.........................
Can you describe something else in the picture?

**S2** I see...........................
What do you think?

**S1** I think.............
Where do you think this is and how do you know?

**S2** I think............
Do you agree or disagree?

**S1** I agree (disagree) because.............
Is there anything else you would like to add about the picture?

**S2** I would like to add............

# Practice Activity #3

**Directions:** Practice having a constructive conversation about the picture:

☐ With a partner ☐ In a small group ☐ With an adult

**S1** *Look at the picture.*
*Describe one thing that you see.*

**S2** *I see..........................*
*What do you see in the picture?*

**S1** *In the picture, I see........................*
*Can you describe something else in the picture?*

**S2** *I see...........................*
*What do you think?*

**S1** *I think.............*
*Where do you think this is and how do you know?*

**S2** *I think............*
*Do you agree or disagree?*

**S1** *I agree (disagree) because..............*
*Is there anything else you would like to add about the picture?*

**S2** *I would like to add...........*

# Practice Activity #4

**Directions:** Practice having a constructive conversation about the picture:

☐ With a partner    ☐ In a small group    ☐ With an adult

**S1** *Look at the picture.*
*Describe one thing that you see.*

**S2** *I see...........................*
*What do you see in the picture?*

**S1** *In the picture, I see.........................*
*Can you describe something else in the picture?*

**S2** *I see...........................*
*What do you think?*

**S1** *I think..............*
*Where do you think this is and how do you know?*

**S2** *I think...........*
*Do you agree or disagree?*

**S1** *I agree (disagree) because..............*
*Is there anything else you would like to add about the picture?*

**S2** *I would like to add...........*

# Practice Activity #5

**Directions:** Practice having a constructive conversation about the picture:

☐ With a partner ☐ In a small group ☐ With an adult

**S1** Look at the picture.
Describe one thing that you see.

**S2** I see...........................
What do you see in the picture?

**S1** In the picture, I see........................
Can you describe something else in the picture?

**S2** I see..........................
What do you think?

**S1** I think..............
Where do you think this is and how do you know?

**S2** I think...........
Do you agree or disagree?

**S1** I agree (disagree) because..............
Is there anything else you would like to add about the picture?

**S2** I would like to add...........

# Speaking
## *Speech Functions*

**This section includes:**
- Guided Activity
- Teacher's ELD Standards Record Sheet
- Student Practice Activities:
  - Constructive Conversations Guide
  - Speech Function Student Practice

- - - - - - - - - - - - - - - - - - - - - - - - - - - - - - - - - - - - - - - - -

**Alignment to CA ELD Standards:**

**Alignment to CCSS:**

**Part I: Interacting in Meaningful Ways**
A.4 Adapting Language Choices
Adapting language choices to various contexts
(based on task, purpose, audience, and text type)

W.3.4–5; SL.3.1, 6; L.3.1, 3, 6
W.4.4–5; SL.4.1, 6; L.4.1, 3, 6
W.5.4–5; SL.5.1, 6; L.5.1, 3, 6

**Part II: Learning About How English Works**
B.3 Expanding & Enriching Ideas
Using verbs and verb phrases

W.3.5; SL.3.6; L.3.1, 3, 6
W.4.5; SL.4.6; L.4.1, 3, 6
W.5.5; SL.5.6; L.5.1, 3, 6

**Part II: Learning About How English Works**
B.4 Expanding & Enriching Ideas
Using nouns and noun phrases

W.3.5; SL.3.6; L.3.1, 3, 6
W.4.5; SL.4.6; L.4.1, 3, 6
W.5.5; SL.5.6; L.5.1, 3, 6

**Part II: Learning About How English Works**
B.5 Expanding & Enriching Ideas
Modifying to add details

W.3.5; SL.3.4, 6; L.3.1, 3, 6
W.4.5; SL.4.4, 6; L.4.1, 3, 6
W.5.5; SL.5.4, 6; L.5.1, 3, 6

- - - - - - - - - - - - - - - - - - - - - - - - - - - - - - - - - - - - - - - - -

**Guided Activities Direction:**
1. Follow the teacher directions.
2. **Say** the **Teacher Script** (indicated by ( SAY ) )
3. Guide students through:
   - Providing responses that clearly addresses the language functions (i.e. asking for information, asking for permission, etc.)
4. Then have students practice with additional speaking activities.

# Guided Activity #1

 **There are no pictures for this activity. I'm going to tell you about a situation that could happen to you. Then, tell me what you would say.**

· · · · · · · · · · · · · · · · · · · · · · · · · · · · · · · · · · · · · · · · · · · · · · · · · · · · · · · · · · · · ·

 **1**

**You want to know when is the class field trip to the zoo. What would you say to your teacher?**

 **2**

**You need an extra day to finish your science project. What would you say to your teacher?**

 **3**

**You want to know if the library has books about polar bears. What would you say to the librarian?**

 **4**

**A book drops out of your friend's backpack. What would you say to your friend?**

 **5**

**The cafeteria is out of apples, but you would like one for your lunch. What would you say to the cafeteria worker?**

# Guided Activity #2

 **SAY** There are no pictures for this activity. I'm going to tell you about a situation that could happen to you. Then, tell me what you would say.

......................................................................

 **SAY** **1**

You need a sharpened pencil for the test. What would you say to your teacher?

 **SAY** **2**

You want to invite your friend over for a party. What would you say to your friend?

 **SAY** **3**

You need to go to the restroom during class. What would you say to your teacher?

 **SAY** **4**

You want to interview the school principal for your essay. What would you say to the principal?

 **SAY** **5**

You want to know if the school bus will stop at First Street. What would you say to the bus driver?

# Guided Activity #3

 **SAY** There are no pictures for this activity. I'm going to tell you about a situation that could happen to you. Then, tell me what you would say.

 **SAY** **1** You want to know when the art project is due. What would you say to your teacher?

 **SAY** **2** You want to invite your friend over to your house to study for the test. What would you say to your friend?

 **SAY** **3** You feel sick and want to go to the school nurse. What would you say to your teacher?

 **SAY** **4** You want to play basketball with your friend for recess. What would you say to your friend?

 **SAY** **5** A student forget their homework on the school bus. What would you say to the bus driver?

# Guided Activity #4

 **SAY** There are no pictures for this activity. I'm going to tell you about a situation that could happen to you. Then, tell me what you would say.

• • • • • • • • • • • • • • • • • • • • • • • • • • • • • • • • • • • • • • • • • • • • •

 **SAY** **1**

The school bus is late and you want to know what time it will arrive. What would you say to your teacher?

 **SAY** **2**

You lost your field trip permission form and need another one. What would you say to your teacher?

 **SAY** **3**

You need to type your essay on the classroom computer during recess. What would you say to your teacher?

 **SAY** **4**

You want to invite your friend to the library to do research for your project. What would you say to your friend?

 **SAY** **5**

The sink in the students' restroom is not working. What would you say to the custodian?

# Guided Activity #5

 **SAY** There are no pictures for this activity. I'm going to tell you about a situation that could happen to you. Then, tell me what you would say.

· · · · · · · · · · · · · · · · · · · · · · · · · · · · · · · · · · · · · · · · · · · · · · · · · · · ·

 **SAY** **1**

You would like an extra day to finish your history essay. What would you say to your teacher?

 **SAY** **2**

You want to borrow a book about the rain forest. What would you say to the librarian?

 **SAY** **3**

You want to offer your friend your extra bag of chips. What would you say to your friend?

 **SAY** **4**

You want to know if Monday is a school holiday. What would you say to your teacher?

 **SAY** **5**

The school play is after school and you want to know what time does it start. What would you say to the principal?

# ELD Standards Record Sheet

Directions:

1. Look at the CA ELD standards (**BELOW**) that correspond to this section.
2. Reference these specific standards for the template Record Sheet.
3. Use the following template Record Sheet to monitor students' proficiency levels for the **GUIDED ACTIVITIES** in this section.
4. Fill out all the information.  Circle, check, highlight the proficiency level. (*There is space for 20 students.  Make additional copies, as needed*)
5. Retain for your records to be used during grading, parent/student conferences, lesson planning, ELD documentation, etc.

 **Suggestion: You can make one copy of each guided activity and/or the student practice sheets and laminate them.  Organize the laminated sheets onto a book ring.  Now it'll be easily accessible for whole group, small group, one-on-one, centers, etc.  Copy as many of the ELD Standards Record Sheet as you need and keep it handy along with the activities**.

# ELD Standards Record Sheet

## CA ELD Standards & Proficiency Levels

**Part I:** Interacting in Meaningful Ways
### *A.4 Adapting Language Choices*

| EMERGING (EM) | EXPANDING (EX) | BRIDGING (BR) |
|---|---|---|
| *Requires **Substantial** Support* | *Requires **Moderate** Support* | *Requires **Light** Support* |
| **GRADE 3** | | |
| • *Recognize that language choices (e.g. vocabulary) vary according to:*<br>   ○ *social setting (e.g. playground vs. classroom)*<br>• *Requires substantial support from peers or adults* | • *Adjust language choices (e.g. vocabulary, use of dialogue, etc.) according to:*<br>   ○ *Purpose (e.g. persuading, entertaining)*<br>   ○ *social setting*<br>   ○ *audience (e.g. peers vs adults)*<br>• *Requires moderate support from peers or adults* | • *Adjust language choices according to:*<br>   ○ *purpose (e.g. persuading, entertaining)*<br>   ○ *Task*<br>   ○ *audience (e.g. peer-to-peer, vs. peer-to-teacher)*<br>• *Requires light support from peers or adults* |
| **GRADE 4** | | |
| • *Adjust language choices according to:*<br>   ○ *social setting (e.g. playground vs. classroom)*<br>   ○ *audience (e.g. peers, teacher)*<br>• *Requires substantial support* | • *Adjust language choices according to:*<br>   ○ *purpose (e.g. persuading, entertaining)*<br>   ○ *task (e.g. telling a story vs explaining a science experiment)*<br>   ○ *audience*<br>• *Requires moderate support* | • *Adjust language choices according to:*<br>   ○ *purpose*<br>   ○ *task (e.g facilitating a science experiment)*<br>   ○ *audience*<br>• *Requires light support* |
| **GRADE 5** | | |
| • *Adjust language choices according to:*<br>   ○ *social setting (e.g.*<br>   ○ *playground vs. classroom)*<br>   ○ *audience (e.g. peers, teacher)*<br>• *Requires substantial support* | • *Adjust language choices according to:*<br>   ○ *purpose (e.g. persuading, entertaining)*<br>   ○ *task (e.g. telling a story vs explaining a science experiment)*<br>   ○ *audience*<br>• *Requires moderate support* | • *Adjust language choices according to:*<br>   ○ *purpose*<br>   ○ *task (e.g facilitating a science experiment)*<br>   ○ *audience*<br>• *Requires light support* |

**Speaking:** *Speech Functions*

# ELD Standards Record Sheet

## CA ELD Standards & Proficiency Levels

**Part II:** Learning About How English Works
### B.3 Using Verbs and Verb Phrases

| EMERGING (EM)→ | EXPANDING (EX) → | BRIDGING (BR) → |
|---|---|---|
| Requires **Substantial** Support | Requires **Moderate** Support | Requires **Light** Support |
| **GRADE 3** | | |
| • Use frequently used verbs<br>• Use different verb types (e.g. doing, saying, being/having, thinking/feeling)<br>• Use different verb tenses (e.g. simple past for recounting an experience)<br>• Appropriate for the text type and discipline to convey time | • Use a _growing number_ of verb types (e.g. doing, saying, being/having, thinking/feeling)<br>• Use a _growing number_ of verb tenses (e.g. simple past for retelling, simple present for a science description)<br>• Appropriate for the text type and discipline to convey time | • Use a _variety_ of verb types (e.g. doing, saying, being/having, thinking/feeling)<br>• Use a _variety_ of verb tenses (e.g. simple present for a science description, simple future to predict)<br>• Appropriate for the text type and discipline to convey time |
| **GRADE 4** | | |
| • Use various verbs<br>• Use various verb types (e.g. doing, saying, being/having, thinking/feeling)<br>• Use various verb tenses (e.g. simple past for recounting an experience)<br>• Appropriate for the text type and discipline for familiar topics | • Use various verbs<br>• Use various verb types (e.g. doing, saying, being/having, thinking/feeling)<br>• Use various verb tenses (e.g. simple past for retelling, timeless present for science explanation)<br>• Appropriate for the _task_, text type and discipline<br>• _For an increasing variety of familiar and new topics_ | • Use various verb<br>• Use various verb types (e.g. doing, saying, being/having, thinking/feeling)<br>• Use various verb tenses(e.g. timeless present for science explanation, mixture of past and present for historical information report)<br>• Appropriate for the task and text type<br>• For a _variety_ of familiar and new topics |
| **GRADE 5** | | |
| • Use frequently used verbs (e.g. take, like, eat)<br>• Use various verb types (e.g. doing, saying, being/having, thinking/feeling)<br>• Use various verb tenses (e.g. simple past for recounting an experience)<br>• Appropriate for the text type and discipline for familiar topics | • Use _various_ verb types (e.g. doing, saying, being/having, thinking/feeling)<br>• Use various verb tenses (e.g. simple past for retelling, timeless present for science a description)<br>• Appropriate for the _task_, text type and discipline<br>• _For an increasing variety of topics_ | • Use various verb types (e.g. doing, saying, being/having, thinking/feeling)<br>• Use various verb tenses (e.g. timeless present for science description, mixture of past and present for narrative or history explanation)<br>• Appropriate for the task and text type<br>• For a _variety_ of topics |

# ELD Standards Record Sheet

## CA ELD Standards & Proficiency Levels

### Part II: Learning About How English Works
### B.4 Using Nouns and Noun Phrases

| EMERGING (EM) ➡ | EXPANDING (EX) ➡ | BRIDGING (BR) |
|---|---|---|
| Requires **Substantial** Support | Requires **Moderate** Support | Requires **Light** Support |
| | **GRADE 3** | • Expand noun phrases in a <u>variety</u> of ways in order to enrich:<br>  ○ The meaning of sentences and<br>  ○ Add details about ideas, people, things, etc. (e.g. adding comparative/superlative adjectives to nouns, simple clause embedding) |
| • Expand noun phrases in simple ways in order to enrich:<br>  ○ The meaning of sentences<br>  ○ Add details about ideas, people, things, etc. (e.g. adding an adjective to a noun) | • Expand noun phrases in a <u>growing number</u> of ways in order to enrich:<br>  ○ The meaning of sentences<br>  ○ Add details about ideas, people, things, etc. (e.g. adding comparative/superlative adjectives to nouns) | |
| | **GRADE 4** | • Expand noun phrases in an <u>increasing variety</u> of ways in order to enrich:<br>  ○ The meaning of sentences and<br>  ○ Add details about ideas, people, things, etc. (e.g. adding general academic adjectives and adverbs to noun phrases or more complex clause embedding) |
| • Expand noun phrases in simple ways in order to enrich:<br>  ○ The meaning of sentences<br>  ○ Add details about ideas, people, things, etc. (e.g. adding an adjective) | • Expand noun phrases in a <u>variety</u> of ways in order to enrich:<br>  ○ The meaning of sentences<br>  ○ Add details about ideas, people, things, etc. (e.g. adding adjectives to noun phrases or simple clause embedding) | |
| | **GRADE 5** | • Expand noun phrases in an <u>increasing variety</u> of ways in order to enrich:<br>  ○ The meaning of sentences<br>  ○ Add details about ideas, people, things, etc. (e.g. adding comparative/superlative and general academic adjectives to noun phrases or more complex clause embedding) |
| • Expand noun phrases in simple ways in order to enrich:<br>  ○ The meaning of sentences<br>  ○ Add details about ideas, people, things, etc. (e.g. adding an adjective to a noun) | • Expand noun phrases in a <u>variety</u> of ways in order to enrich:<br>  ○ The meaning of sentences<br>  ○ Add details about ideas, people, things, etc. (e.g. adding comparative/superlative adjectives to noun phrases or simple clause embedding) | |

# ELD Standards Record Sheet

## CA ELD Standards & Proficiency Levels

**Part II:** Learning About How English Works
### *B.5 Modifying to Add Details*

| EMERGING (EM)→ | ➤ EXPANDING (EX) → | ➤ BRIDGING (BR) |
|---|---|---|
| *Requires **Substantial** Support* | *Requires **Moderate** Support* | *Requires **Light** Support* |
| **GRADE 3** | | |
| • *Expand sentences with adverbials (e.g. adverbs, adverb phrases, prepositional phrases)*<br>• *Use these to provide details about a familiar activity or process (e.g. time, manner, place, cause) (e.g. They walked to the soccer field.)* | • *Expand sentences with adverbials (e.g. adverbs, adverb phrases, prepositional phrases)*<br>• *Use these to provide details about a familiar or <u>new activity</u> or process (e.g. time, manner, place, cause) (e.g. They worked quietly; They ran across the soccer field.)* | • *Expand sentences with adverbials (e.g. adverbs, adverb phrases, prepositional phrases)*<br>• *Use these to provide details about a <u>range</u> of familiar and new activities or processes. (e.g. time, manner, place, cause) (e.g. They worked quietly all night in their room.)* |
| **GRADE 4** | | |
| • *Expand sentences with familiar adverbials (e.g. basic prepositional phrases)*<br>• *Use these to provide details about a familiar activity or process (e.g. time, manner, place, cause) (e.g. They walked to the soccer field.)* | • *Expand sentences with a <u>growing variety</u> of adverbials (e.g. adverbs, prepositional phrases)*<br>• *Use these to provide details about a familiar or <u>new activity</u> or process (e.g. time, manner, place, cause) (e.g. They worked quietly; They ran across the soccer field.)* | • *Expand sentences with a <u>variety</u> of adverbials (e.g. adverbs, adverb phrases, prepositional phrases)*<br>• *Use these to provide details about a <u>variety</u> of familiar and new activities or processes.(e.g. time, manner, place, cause) (e.g. They worked quietly all night in their room.)* |
| **GRADE 5** | | |
| • *Expand and enrich sentences with adverbials (e.g. adverbs, adverb phrases, prepositional phrases)*<br>• *Use these to provide details about a familiar activity or process (e.g. time, manner, place, cause)* | • *Expand and enrich sentences with adverbials (e.g. adverbs, adverb phrases, prepositional phrases)*<br>• *Use these to provide details about a familiar or <u>new activity</u> or process (e.g. time, manner, place, cause)* | • *Expand and enrich sentences with adverbials (e.g. adverbs, adverb phrases, prepositional phrases)*<br>• *Use these to provide details about a <u>variety</u> of familiar and new activities or processes.(e.g. time, manner, place, cause)* |

# ELD Standards Record Sheet

**Teacher:** _____ **Class:** _____

**Standards:** *PI.A.4*  **Guided Activities and Proficiency Levels:**

| Students: | #1 | #2 | #3 | #4 | #5 |
|---|---|---|---|---|---|
| _____ | EM / EX / BR | EM / EX / BR | EM / EX / BR | EM / EX / BR | EM / EX / BR |
| _____ | EM / EX / BR | EM / EX / BR | EM / EX / BR | EM / EX / BR | EM / EX / BR |
| _____ | EM / EX / BR | EM / EX / BR | EM / EX / BR | EM / EX / BR | EM / EX / BR |
| _____ | EM / EX / BR | EM / EX / BR | EM / EX / BR | EM / EX / BR | EM / EX / BR |
| _____ | EM / EX / BR | EM / EX / BR | EM / EX / BR | EM / EX / BR | EM / EX / BR |
| _____ | EM / EX / BR | EM / EX / BR | EM / EX / BR | EM / EX / BR | EM / EX / BR |
| _____ | EM / EX / BR | EM / EX / BR | EM / EX / BR | EM / EX / BR | EM / EX / BR |
| _____ | EM / EX / BR | EM / EX / BR | EM / EX / BR | EM / EX / BR | EM / EX / BR |
| _____ | EM / EX / BR | EM / EX / BR | EM / EX / BR | EM / EX / BR | EM / EX / BR |
| _____ | EM / EX / BR | EM / EX / BR | EM / EX / BR | EM / EX / BR | EM / EX / BR |
| _____ | EM / EX / BR | EM / EX / BR | EM / EX / BR | EM / EX / BR | EM / EX / BR |
| _____ | EM / EX / BR | EM / EX / BR | EM / EX / BR | EM / EX / BR | EM / EX / BR |
| _____ | EM / EX / BR | EM / EX / BR | EM / EX / BR | EM / EX / BR | EM / EX / BR |
| _____ | EM / EX / BR | EM / EX / BR | EM / EX / BR | EM / EX / BR | EM / EX / BR |
| _____ | EM / EX / BR | EM / EX / BR | EM / EX / BR | EM / EX / BR | EM / EX / BR |
| _____ | EM / EX / BR | EM / EX / BR | EM / EX / BR | EM / EX / BR | EM / EX / BR |
| _____ | EM / EX / BR | EM / EX / BR | EM / EX / BR | EM / EX / BR | EM / EX / BR |
| _____ | EM / EX / BR | EM / EX / BR | EM / EX / BR | EM / EX / BR | EM / EX / BR |
| _____ | EM / EX / BR | EM / EX / BR | EM / EX / BR | EM / EX / BR | EM / EX / BR |

**Speaking:** *Speech Functions*

# ELD Standards Record Sheet

**Teacher:** _____  **Class:** _____

**Standards**: *PII.B.3*          **Guided Activities and Proficiency Levels:**

| Students: | #1 | #2 | #3 | #4 | #5 |
|---|---|---|---|---|---|
| | EM / EX / BR | EM / EX / BR | EM / EX / BR | EM / EX / BR | EM / EX / BR |
| | EM / EX / BR | EM / EX / BR | EM / EX / BR | EM / EX / BR | EM / EX / BR |
| | EM / EX / BR | EM / EX / BR | EM / EX / BR | EM / EX / BR | EM / EX / BR |
| | EM / EX / BR | EM / EX / BR | EM / EX / BR | EM / EX / BR | EM / EX / BR |
| | EM / EX / BR | EM / EX / BR | EM / EX / BR | EM / EX / BR | EM / EX / BR |
| | EM / EX / BR | EM / EX / BR | EM / EX / BR | EM / EX / BR | EM / EX / BR |
| | EM / EX / BR | EM / EX / BR | EM / EX / BR | EM / EX / BR | EM / EX / BR |
| | EM / EX / BR | EM / EX / BR | EM / EX / BR | EM / EX / BR | EM / EX / BR |
| | EM / EX / BR | EM / EX / BR | EM / EX / BR | EM / EX / BR | EM / EX / BR |
| | EM / EX / BR | EM / EX / BR | EM / EX / BR | EM / EX / BR | EM / EX / BR |
| | EM / EX / BR | EM / EX / BR | EM / EX / BR | EM / EX / BR | EM / EX / BR |
| | EM / EX / BR | EM / EX / BR | EM / EX / BR | EM / EX / BR | EM / EX / BR |
| | EM / EX / BR | EM / EX / BR | EM / EX / BR | EM / EX / BR | EM / EX / BR |
| | EM / EX / BR | EM / EX / BR | EM / EX / BR | EM / EX / BR | EM / EX / BR |
| | EM / EX / BR | EM / EX / BR | EM / EX / BR | EM / EX / BR | EM / EX / BR |
| | EM / EX / BR | EM / EX / BR | EM / EX / BR | EM / EX / BR | EM / EX / BR |
| | EM / EX / BR | EM / EX / BR | EM / EX / BR | EM / EX / BR | EM / EX / BR |
| | EM / EX / BR | EM / EX / BR | EM / EX / BR | EM / EX / BR | EM / EX / BR |
| | EM / EX / BR | EM / EX / BR | EM / EX / BR | EM / EX / BR | EM / EX / BR |
| | EM / EX / BR | EM / EX / BR | EM / EX / BR | EM / EX / BR | EM / EX / BR |

# ELD Standards Record Sheet

**Teacher:** _____  **Class:** _____

**Standards**: *PII.B.4*

**Guided Activities and Proficiency Levels:**

| Students: | #1 | #2 | #3 | #4 | #5 |
|---|---|---|---|---|---|
| _____ | EM / EX / BR | EM / EX / BR | EM / EX / BR | EM / EX / BR | EM / EX / BR |
| _____ | EM / EX / BR | EM / EX / BR | EM / EX / BR | EM / EX / BR | EM / EX / BR |
| _____ | EM / EX / BR | EM / EX / BR | EM / EX / BR | EM / EX / BR | EM / EX / BR |
| _____ | EM / EX / BR | EM / EX / BR | EM / EX / BR | EM / EX / BR | EM / EX / BR |
| _____ | EM / EX / BR | EM / EX / BR | EM / EX / BR | EM / EX / BR | EM / EX / BR |
| _____ | EM / EX / BR | EM / EX / BR | EM / EX / BR | EM / EX / BR | EM / EX / BR |
| _____ | EM / EX / BR | EM / EX / BR | EM / EX / BR | EM / EX / BR | EM / EX / BR |
| _____ | EM / EX / BR | EM / EX / BR | EM / EX / BR | EM / EX / BR | EM / EX / BR |
| _____ | EM / EX / BR | EM / EX / BR | EM / EX / BR | EM / EX / BR | EM / EX / BR |
| _____ | EM / EX / BR | EM / EX / BR | EM / EX / BR | EM / EX / BR | EM / EX / BR |
| _____ | EM / EX / BR | EM / EX / BR | EM / EX / BR | EM / EX / BR | EM / EX / BR |
| _____ | EM / EX / BR | EM / EX / BR | EM / EX / BR | EM / EX / BR | EM / EX / BR |
| _____ | EM / EX / BR | EM / EX / BR | EM / EX / BR | EM / EX / BR | EM / EX / BR |
| _____ | EM / EX / BR | EM / EX / BR | EM / EX / BR | EM / EX / BR | EM / EX / BR |
| _____ | EM / EX / BR | EM / EX / BR | EM / EX / BR | EM / EX / BR | EM / EX / BR |
| _____ | EM / EX / BR | EM / EX / BR | EM / EX / BR | EM / EX / BR | EM / EX / BR |
| _____ | EM / EX / BR | EM / EX / BR | EM / EX / BR | EM / EX / BR | EM / EX / BR |
| _____ | EM / EX / BR | EM / EX / BR | EM / EX / BR | EM / EX / BR | EM / EX / BR |
| _____ | EM / EX / BR | EM / EX / BR | EM / EX / BR | EM / EX / BR | EM / EX / BR |
| _____ | EM / EX / BR | EM / EX / BR | EM / EX / BR | EM / EX / BR | EM / EX / BR |

# ELD Standards Record Sheet

**Teacher:** _____  **Class:** _____

**Standards**: *PII.B.5*  **Guided Activities and Proficiency Levels:**

| Students: | #1 | #2 | #3 | #4 | #5 |
|---|---|---|---|---|---|
| | EM / EX / BR | EM / EX / BR | EM / EX / BR | EM / EX / BR | EM / EX / BR |
| | EM / EX / BR | EM / EX / BR | EM / EX / BR | EM / EX / BR | EM / EX / BR |
| | EM / EX / BR | EM / EX / BR | EM / EX / BR | EM / EX / BR | EM / EX / BR |
| | EM / EX / BR | EM / EX / BR | EM / EX / BR | EM / EX / BR | EM / EX / BR |
| | EM / EX / BR | EM / EX / BR | EM / EX / BR | EM / EX / BR | EM / EX / BR |
| | EM / EX / BR | EM / EX / BR | EM / EX / BR | EM / EX / BR | EM / EX / BR |
| | EM / EX / BR | EM / EX / BR | EM / EX / BR | EM / EX / BR | EM / EX / BR |
| | EM / EX / BR | EM / EX / BR | EM / EX / BR | EM / EX / BR | EM / EX / BR |
| | EM / EX / BR | EM / EX / BR | EM / EX / BR | EM / EX / BR | EM / EX / BR |
| | EM / EX / BR | EM / EX / BR | EM / EX / BR | EM / EX / BR | EM / EX / BR |
| | EM / EX / BR | EM / EX / BR | EM / EX / BR | EM / EX / BR | EM / EX / BR |
| | EM / EX / BR | EM / EX / BR | EM / EX / BR | EM / EX / BR | EM / EX / BR |
| | EM / EX / BR | EM / EX / BR | EM / EX / BR | EM / EX / BR | EM / EX / BR |
| | EM / EX / BR | EM / EX / BR | EM / EX / BR | EM / EX / BR | EM / EX / BR |
| | EM / EX / BR | EM / EX / BR | EM / EX / BR | EM / EX / BR | EM / EX / BR |
| | EM / EX / BR | EM / EX / BR | EM / EX / BR | EM / EX / BR | EM / EX / BR |
| | EM / EX / BR | EM / EX / BR | EM / EX / BR | EM / EX / BR | EM / EX / BR |
| | EM / EX / BR | EM / EX / BR | EM / EX / BR | EM / EX / BR | EM / EX / BR |
| | EM / EX / BR | EM / EX / BR | EM / EX / BR | EM / EX / BR | EM / EX / BR |

# Practice Activities

------------------------------------------------

It is crucial to guide students in having **Constructive Conversations** utilizing skills and strategies that help them develop into productive thinkers and speakers.

- Help students **formulate** their ideas and thinking.
- Help students **explain and extend** their thinking so that it's clear and concise.
- Help students **support** their ideas and thinking with relevant support and information (i.e. from the picture).
- Help students **engage** in constructive dialogue with others through understanding, listening, and **consensus**.

------------------------------------------------

**Practice Activities Direction:**

1. Students can work with partners, small group, or with an adult.

2. Students take turns using the script to help guide them through appropriately addressing the language functions.

3. Students follow turn-taking protocols to build their oral language.

**Speaker #1**'s script is indicated by    **S1**

**Speaker #2**'s script is indicated by  **S2**

# Practice Activity #1

**Directions:** Practice reading the speech functions:

☐ With a partner     ☐ In a small group     ☐ With an adult

**S1**

*You want to know if the class is having a holiday party tomorrow. What would you say to your teacher?*

**S2** *Are we...........................?*

**S2**

*You need an extra copy of the math assignment. What would you say to your teacher?*

**S1**

*May I have...........................?*

**S1**

*You want to invite your friend over for a movie. What would you say to your friend?*

**S2** *Do you want to.........................?*

**S2**

*You want to invite your friend to play soccer during lunch. What would you say to your friend?*

**S1**

*Do you want to.........................?*

# Practice Activity #2

**Directions:** Practice reading the speech functions:

☐ With a partner          ☐ In a small group          ☐ With an adult

**S1**
*You need to borrow your friends cell phone to call your parents. What would you say to your friend?*

**S2**
*May I borrow...........................?*

**S2**
*You want to know if the school bus stops at Grape Street. What would you say to the bus driver?*

**S1**
*Does the bus..........................?*

**S1**
*You want to invite your friend over dinner. What would you say to your friend?*

**S2**
*Do you want to.........................?*

**S2**
*You lost your pencil and need another one. What would you say to your teacher?*

**S1**
*May I have.........................?*

# Practice Activity #3

**Directions:** Practice reading the speech functions:

☐ With a partner ☐ In a small group ☐ With an adult

**S1**

*A library book falls out of your friend's backpack. What would you say to your friend?*

**S2** *You dropped..........................*

**S2**

*You want to know if you can turn in your assignment tomorrow. What would you say to your teacher?*

**S1** *May I..........................?*

**S1**

*The principal is in a meeting and you want to know when she'll be done. What would you say to the secretary?*

**S2** *When will.........................?*

**S2**

*You need help with a math word problem. What would you say to your teacher?*

**S1** *Can you.........................?*

# Practice Activity #4

**Directions:** Practice reading the speech functions:

☐ With a partner     ☐ In a small group     ☐ With an adult

**S1**

*You want to know if the teacher needs help during recess. What would you say to your teacher?*

**S2**

*Do you ...........................?*

**S2**

*You want to know what time the library will be closed. What would you say to the librarian?*

**S1**

*When does.........................?*

**S1**

*You want to play soccer with your friend after school. What would you say to your friend?*

**S2**

*Do you want......................?*

**S2**

*You need a new eraser. What would you say to your teacher?*

**S1**

*May I.........................?*

# Practice Activity #5

**Directions:** Practice reading the speech functions:

☐ With a partner   ☐ In a small group   ☐ With an adult

**S1**

*The equipment room is closed and you want to get a basketball. What would you say to the yard supervisor?*

**S2**

*Can I get.........................?*

**S2**

*You want to know if the library has books about the solar system. What would you say to the librarian?*

**S1**

*Does the library.........................?*

**S1**

*You want to invite your friend over to play video games. What would you say to your friend?*

**S2**

*Would you like to......................?*

**S2**

*You need an extra day to finish your english assignment. What would you say to your teacher?*

**S1**

*May I have.........................?*

# Speaking
## *Support an Opinion*

**This section includes:**
- Guided Activities
- Teacher's ELD Standards Record Sheet
- Student Practice Activities:
  - Constructive Conversations Guide
  - Support an Opinion Student Practice

---

**Alignment to CA ELD Standards:**

**Alignment to CCSS:**

**Part I: Interacting in Meaningful Ways**
C.11 Supporting Opinions
Supporting own opinions and evaluating others' opinions in speaking and writing

W.3.1, 4, 10; SL.3.4, 6; L.3.1–3, 6
W.4.1, 4, 9–10; SL.4.4, 6; L.4.1–3, 6
W.5.1, 4, 9–10; SL.5.4, 6; L.5.1–3, 6

**Part II: Learning About How English Works**
B.3 Expanding & Enriching Ideas
Using verbs and verb phrases

W.3.5; SL.3.6; L.3.1, 3, 6
W.4.5; SL.4.6; L.4.1, 3, 6
W.5.5; SL.5.6; L.5.1, 3, 6

**Part II: Learning About How English Works**
B.4 Expanding & Enriching Ideas
Using nouns and noun phrases

W.3.5; SL.3.6; L.3.1, 3, 6
W.4.5; SL.4.6; L.4.1, 3, 6
W.5.5; SL.5.6; L.5.1, 3, 6

**Part II: Learning About How English Works**
B.5 Expanding & Enriching Ideas
Modifying to add details

W.3.5; SL.3.4, 6; L.3.1, 3, 6
W.4.5; SL.4.4, 6; L.4.1, 3, 6
W.5.5; SL.5.4, 6; L.5.1, 3, 6

**Part II: Learning About How English Works**
C.6 Expanding & Enriching Ideas
Connecting Ideas

W.3.1-3, 5; SL.3.4, 6; L.3.1, 3, 6
W.4.1–3, 5; SL.4.4, 6; L.4.1, 3, 6
W.5.1–3, 5; SL.5.4, 6; L.5.1, 3, 6

---

**Guided Activities Direction:**
1. Show students the pictures.
2. Follow the teacher directions.
3. **Say** the **Teacher Script** (indicated by  )
4. Guide students through:
   - Providing a supported opinion using effective language and relevant reasons
5. Then have students practice with additional speaking activities.

# Guided Activity #1

 **SAY**

Show the student the two pictures.

**I'm going to ask you for your opinion.**

 **SAY**

**Your class will have reading time after lunch. The class will be reading the chapter book.**

**1** **Would it be better to read the chapter book with the teacher or by yourself?**

Point to the picture at the appropriate time while reading the question.

Wait for initial response.

 **SAY**

**Explain your choice by giving relevant reasons to support your opinion.**

**2** Ask the student to support their opinion with relevant reasons.

# Guided Activity #2

 **SAY** Show the student the two pictures.

**I'm going to ask you for your opinion.**

 **SAY**

**Your class will have free time at the end of the day. The teacher gave a choice of playing basketball or soccer.**

**1** **Would it be better for the class to play basketball or soccer during free time?**

Point to the picture at the appropriate time while reading the question.

Wait for initial response.

 **SAY**

**Explain your choice by giving relevant reasons to support your opinion.**

**2** Ask the student to support their opinion with relevant reasons.

# Guided Activity #3

 **SAY** Show the student the two pictures.

**I'm going to ask you for your opinion.**

 **SAY** **Your class has been learning about the solar system. Your class will be making solar system models.**

**1** **Would it be better to work on the project with a partner or by yourself?**

Point to the picture at the appropriate time while reading the question.

Wait for initial response.

 **SAY** **Explain your choice by giving relevant reasons to support your opinion.**

**2** Ask the student to support their opinion with relevant reasons.

# Guided Activity #4

 **SAY**  Show the student the two pictures.

**I'm going to ask you for your opinion.**

 **SAY**

**Your class has been learning about animals. The class will be writing an essay about animals.**

**1  Would it be better to write your essay about animals on a computer or on paper?**

Point to the picture at the appropriate time while reading the question.

Wait for initial response.

 **SAY**

**Explain your choice by giving relevant reasons to support your opinion.**

**2**  Ask the student to support their opinion with relevant reasons.

# Guided Activity #5

 Show the student the two pictures.

**I'm going to ask you for your opinion.**

 **Your class is learning about dinosaurs. Your class will get a choice between watching a movie or reading a book.**

| 1 | **Would it be better to watch a movie or read a book about dinosaurs?** |

Point to the picture at the appropriate time while reading the question.

Wait for initial response.

 **Explain your choice by giving relevant reasons to support your opinion.**

| 2 | Ask the student to support their opinion with relevant reasons. |

**Speaking:** *Supporting an Opinion*

# ELD Standards Record Sheet

<u>Directions:</u>

1. Look at the CA ELD standards (**BELOW**) that correspond to this section.
2. Reference these specific standards for the template Record Sheet.
3. Use the following template Record Sheet to monitor students' proficiency levels for the **GUIDED ACTIVITIES** in this section.
4. Fill out all the information. Circle, check, highlight the proficiency level. (*There is space for 20 students. Make additional copies, as needed*)
5. Retain for your records to be used during grading, parent/student conferences, lesson planning, ELD documentation, etc.

 **Suggestion: You can make one copy of each guided activity and/or the student practice sheets and laminate them. Organize the laminated sheets onto a book ring. Now it'll be easily accessible for whole group, small group, one-on-one, centers, etc. Copy as many of the ELD Standards Record Sheet as you need and keep it handy along with the activities**.

# ELD Standards Record Sheet

## CA ELD Standards & Proficiency Levels
### Part I: Interacting in Meaningful Ways
### *C.11 Supporting Opinions*

| EMERGING (EM) ➤ | EXPANDING (EX) ➤ | BRIDGING (BR) |
|---|---|---|
| Requires **Substantial** Support | Requires **Moderate** Support | Requires **Light** Support |
| | **GRADE 3** | • Support opinions or persuade others by providing:<br>   ○ good reasons<br>   ○ <u>detailed</u> textual evidence<br>   ○ relevant background knowledge about the content (e.g. specific evidence or graphics from text) |
| • Support opinions by providing:<br>   ○ good reasons<br>   ○ some textual evidence<br>   ○ relevant background knowledge (e.g. referring to textual evidence or knowledge of content) | • Support opinions by providing:<br>   ○ good reasons<br>   ○ <u>increasingly detailed</u> textual evidence<br>   ○ relevant background knowledge <u>about the content</u> (e.g. providing examples from the text) | |
| | **GRADE 4** | • Support opinions or persuade others by expressing appropriate/accurate reasons using:<br>   ○ <u>Detailed</u> textual evidence (e.g. Quotations or specific events from text)<br>   ○ relevant background knowledge about content<br>• Requires <u>light</u> support<br>• Express attitude and opinions or temper statements with <u>nuanced</u> modal expressions (e.g. probably/certainly, should/would) and paraphrasing (e.g. In my opinion...) |
| • Support opinions by expressing appropriate/accurate reasons using:<br>   ○ textual evidence (e.g. referring to text)<br>   ○ relevant background knowledge about content<br>• Requires substantial support<br>• Express ideas and opinions or expressions (e.g. can, will, maybe) | • Support opinions or <u>persuade others</u> by expressing appropriate/accurate reasons using:<br>   ○ <u>Some</u> textual evidence (e.g. Paraphrasing facts)<br>   ○ relevant background knowledge <u>about content</u><br>• Requires <u>moderate</u> support<br>• Express <u>attitude</u> and opinions or <u>temper statements with familiar modal expressions</u> (e.g. maybe/probably, can/must) | |
| | **GRADE 5** | • Support opinions or persuade others by expressing appropriate/accurate reasons using:<br>   ○ <u>Detailed</u> textual evidence (e.g. Quotations or specific events from text)<br>• relevant background knowledge about content<br>• Requires <u>light</u> support<br>• Express attitude and opinions or temper statements with <u>nuanced modal expressions</u> (e.g. probably/certainly, should/would) and paraphrasing (e.g. In my opinion...) |
| • Support opinions by expressing appropriate/accurate reasons using:<br>   ○ textual evidence (e.g. referring to text)<br>   ○ relevant background knowledge about content<br>• Requires substantial support<br>• Express ideas and opinions or expressions (e.g. can, will, maybe) | • Support opinions or <u>persuade others</u> by expressing appropriate/accurate reasons using:<br>   ○ <u>Some</u> textual evidence (e.g. Paraphrasing facts)<br>• relevant background knowledge <u>about content</u><br>• Requires <u>moderate</u> support<br>• Express <u>attitude</u> and opinions or <u>temper statements with familiar modal expressions</u> (e.g. maybe/probably, can/must) | |

# ELD Standards Record Sheet

## CA ELD Standards & Proficiency Levels

**Part II:** Learning About How English Works
### B.3 Using Verbs and Verb Phrases

| EMERGING (EM) → | EXPANDING (EX) → | BRIDGING (BR) → |
|---|---|---|
| Requires **Substantial** Support | Requires **Moderate** Support | Requires **Light** Support |
| **GRADE 3** | | |
| • Use frequently used verbs<br>• Use different verb types (e.g. doing, saying, being/having, thinking/feeling)<br>• Use different verb tenses (e.g. simple past for recounting an experience)<br>• Appropriate for the text type and discipline to convey time | • Use a <u>growing number</u> of verb types (e.g. doing, saying, being/having, thinking/feeling)<br>• Use a <u>growing number</u> of verb tenses (e.g. simple past for retelling, simple present for a science description)<br>• Appropriate for the text type and discipline to convey time | • Use a <u>variety</u> of verb types (e.g. doing, saying, being/having, thinking/feeling)<br>• Use a <u>variety</u> of verb tenses (e.g. simple present for a science description, simple future to predict)<br>• Appropriate for the text type and discipline to convey time |
| **GRADE 4** | | |
| • Use various verbs<br>• Use various verb types (e.g. doing, saying, being/having, thinking/feeling)<br>• Use various verb tenses (e.g. simple past for recounting an experience)<br>• Appropriate for the text type and discipline for familiar topics | • Use various verbs<br>• Use various verb types (e.g. doing, saying, being/having, thinking/feeling)<br>• Use various verb tenses (e.g. simple past for retelling, timeless present for science explanation)<br>• Appropriate for the <u>task</u>, text type and discipline<br>• <u>For an increasing variety of familiar and new topics</u> | • Use various verb<br>• Use various verb types (e.g. doing, saying, being/having, thinking/feeling)<br>• Use various verb tenses(e.g. timeless present for science explanation, mixture of past and present for historical information report)<br>• Appropriate for the task and text type<br>• For a <u>variety</u> of familiar and new topics |
| **GRADE 5** | | |
| • Use frequently used verbs (e.g. take, like, eat)<br>• Use various verb types (e.g. doing, saying, being/having, thinking/feeling)<br>• Use various verb tenses (e.g. simple past for recounting an experience)<br>• Appropriate for the text type and discipline for familiar topics | • Use <u>various</u> verb types (e.g. doing, saying, being/having, thinking/feeling)<br>• Use various verb tenses (e.g. simple past for retelling, timeless present for science a description)<br>• Appropriate for the <u>task</u>, text type and discipline<br>• <u>For an increasing variety of topics</u> | • Use various verb types (e.g. doing, saying, being/having, thinking/feeling)<br>• Use various verb tenses (e.g. timeless present for science description, mixture of past and present for narrative or history explanation)<br>• Appropriate for the task and text type<br>• For a <u>variety</u> of topics |

# ELD Standards Record Sheet

## CA ELD Standards & Proficiency Levels

**Part II:** Learning About How English Works
### *B.4 Using Nouns and Noun Phrases*

| EMERGING (EM) | EXPANDING (EX) | BRIDGING (BR) |
|---|---|---|
| *Requires **Substantial** Support* | *Requires **Moderate** Support* | *Requires **Light** Support* |
| | **GRADE 3** | • *Expand noun phrases in a <u>variety</u> of ways in order to enrich:* |
| • *Expand noun phrases in simple ways in order to enrich:* | • *Expand noun phrases in a <u>growing number</u> of ways in order to enrich:* | ◦ *The meaning of sentences and* |
| ◦ *The meaning of sentences* | ◦ *The meaning of sentences* | ◦ *Add details about ideas, people, things, etc. (e.g. adding comparative/superlative adjectives to nouns, simple clause embedding)* |
| ◦ *Add details about ideas, people, things, etc. (e.g. adding an adjective to a noun)* | ◦ *Add details about ideas, people, things, etc. (e.g. adding comparative/superlative adjectives to nouns)* | |
| | **GRADE 4** | • *Expand noun phrases in an <u>increasing variety</u> of ways in order to enrich:* |
| • *Expand noun phrases in simple ways in order to enrich:* | • *Expand noun phrases in a <u>variety</u> of ways in order to enrich:* | ◦ *The meaning of sentences and* |
| ◦ *The meaning of sentences* | ◦ *The meaning of sentences* | ◦ *Add details about ideas, people, things, etc. (e.g. adding general academic adjectives and adverbs to noun phrases or more complex clause embedding)* |
| ◦ *Add details about ideas, people, things, etc. (e.g. adding an adjective)* | ◦ *Add details about ideas, people, things, etc. (e.g. adding adjectives to noun phrases or simple clause embedding)* | |
| | **GRADE 5** | • *Expand noun phrases in an <u>increasing variety</u> of ways in order to enrich:* |
| • *Expand noun phrases in simple ways in order to enrich:* | • *Expand noun phrases in a <u>variety</u> of ways in order to enrich:* | ◦ *The meaning of sentences* |
| ◦ *The meaning of sentences* | ◦ *The meaning of sentences* | ◦ *Add details about ideas, people, things, etc. (e.g. adding comparative/superlative and general academic adjectives to noun phrases or more complex clause embedding)* |
| ◦ *Add details about ideas, people, things, etc. (e.g. adding an adjective to a noun)* | ◦ *Add details about ideas, people, things, etc. (e.g. adding comparative/superlative adjectives to noun phrases or simple clause embedding)* | |

**Speaking:** *Supporting an Opinion*

# ELD Standards Record Sheet

## CA ELD Standards & Proficiency Levels

**Part II:** Learning About How English Works
### *B.5 Modifying to Add Details*

| EMERGING (EM) ➔ | EXPANDING (EX) ➔ | BRIDGING (BR) |
|---|---|---|
| Requires **Substantial** Support | Requires **Moderate** Support | Requires **Light** Support |
| **GRADE 3** | | |
| • *Expand sentences with adverbials (e.g. adverbs, adverb phrases, prepositional phrases)*<br>• *Use these to provide details about a familiar activity or process (e.g. time, manner, place, cause) (e.g. They walked to the soccer field.)* | • *Expand sentences with adverbials (e.g. adverbs, adverb phrases, prepositional phrases)*<br>• *Use these to provide details about a familiar or <u>new activity</u> or process (e.g. time, manner, place, cause) (e.g. They worked quietly; They ran across the soccer field.)* | • *Expand sentences with adverbials (e.g. adverbs, adverb phrases, prepositional phrases)*<br>• *Use these to provide details about a <u>range</u> of familiar and new activities or processes. (e.g. time, manner, place, cause) (e.g. They worked quietly all night in their room.)* |
| **GRADE 4** | | |
| • *Expand sentences with familiar adverbials (e.g. basic prepositional phrases)*<br>• *Use these to provide details about a familiar activity or process (e.g. time, manner, place, cause) (e.g. They walked to the soccer field.)* | • *Expand sentences with a <u>growing variety</u> of adverbials (e.g. adverbs, prepositional phrases)*<br>• *Use these to provide details about a familiar or <u>new activity</u> or process (e.g. time, manner, place, cause) (e.g. They worked quietly; They ran across the soccer field.)* | • *Expand sentences with a <u>variety</u> of adverbials (e.g. adverbs, adverb phrases, prepositional phrases)*<br>• *Use these to provide details about a <u>variety</u> of familiar and new activities or processes.(e.g. time, manner, place, cause) (e.g. They worked quietly all night in their room.)* |
| **GRADE 5** | | |
| • *Expand and enrich sentences with adverbials (e.g. adverbs, adverb phrases, prepositional phrases)*<br>• *Use these to provide details about a familiar activity or process (e.g. time, manner, place, cause)* | • *Expand and enrich sentences with adverbials (e.g. adverbs, adverb phrases, prepositional phrases)*<br>• *Use these to provide details about a familiar or <u>new activity</u> or process (e.g. time, manner, place, cause)* | • *Expand and enrich sentences with adverbials (e.g. adverbs, adverb phrases, prepositional phrases)*<br>• *Use these to provide details about a <u>variety</u> of familiar and new activities or processes.(e.g. time, manner, place, cause)* |

**Speaking:** *Supporting an Opinion*

# ELD Standards Record Sheet
## CA ELD Standards & Proficiency Levels
### **Part II:** Learning About How English Works
### *C.6 Connecting Ideas*

| EMERGING (EM) → | EXPANDING (EX) → | BRIDGING (BR) |
|---|---|---|
| *Requires **Substantial** Support* | *Requires **Moderate** Support* | *Requires **Light** Support* |
| **GRADE 3** | | |
| • *Combine clauses in a few basic ways*<br>• *To make connections between and to join ideas (e.g. creating compound sentences using and, but, so)* | • *Combine clauses in an <u>increasing variety</u> of ways (e.g. creating compound and complex sentences)*<br>• *to make connections between and to join ideas, for example:*<br>　◦ *<u>to express cause/effect (e.g. The deer ran because the mountain lion came.)</u>*<br>　◦ *<u>to make a concession (e.g. She studied all night even though she wasn't feeling well.)</u>* | • *Combine clauses in a <u>wide variety</u> of ways (e.g. creating compound and complex sentences)*<br>• *to make connections between and to join ideas, for example:*<br>　◦ *to express cause/effect (e.g. The deer ran because the mountain lion approached them.)*<br>　◦ *to make a concession(e.g. She studied all night even though she wasn't feeling well.)*<br>　◦ *<u>to link two ideas that happen at the same time (e.g. The cubs played while their mother hunted.)</u>* |
| **GRADE 4** | | |
| • *Combine clauses in a few basic ways*<br>• *To make connections between and to join ideas in sentences (e.g. creating compound sentences using coordinate conjunctions, such as and, but, so)* | • *Combine clauses in an <u>increasing variety</u> of ways (e.g. creating complex sentences using familiar subordinate conjunctions)*<br>• *to make connections between and to join ideas in sentences, for example:*<br>　◦ *<u>to express cause/effect (e.g. The deer ran because the mountain lion came.)</u>*<br>　◦ *<u>to make a concession (e.g. She studied all night even though she wasn't feeling well.)</u>* | • *Combine clauses in a <u>wide variety</u> of ways (e.g. creating complex sentences using a variety of subordinate conjunctions)*<br>• *to make connections between and to join ideas, for example:*<br>　◦ *to express cause/effect (e.g. Since the lion was at the waterhole, the deer ran away.)*<br>　◦ *to make a concession*<br>　◦ *<u>to link two ideas that happen at the same time (e.g. The cubs played while their mother hunted.)</u>* |
| **GRADE 5** | | |
| • *Combine clauses in a few basic ways*<br>• *To make connections between and to join ideas*<br>• *To provide evidence to support ideas or opinions (e.g. You must X because X.)(e.g. creating compound sentences using and, but, so)* | • *Combine clauses in an <u>increasing variety</u> of ways (e.g. creating compound and complex sentences)*<br>• *to make connections between and to join ideas, for example:*<br>　◦ *<u>to express cause/effect (e.g. The deer ran because the mountain lion came.)</u>*<br>　◦ *<u>to make a concession(e.g. She studied all night even though she wasn't feeling well.)</u>*<br>• *To provide reasons to support ideas (e.g. X is an extremely good book because X)* | • *Combine clauses in a <u>wide variety</u> of ways (e.g. creating compound and complex sentences)*<br>• *to make connections between and to join ideas, for example:*<br>　◦ *to express cause/effect (e.g. The deer ran because the mountain lion approached them.)*<br>　◦ *to make a concession (e.g. She studied all night even though she wasn't feeling well.)*<br>　◦ *<u>to link two ideas that happen at the same time (e.g. The cubs played while their mother hunted.)</u>*<br>• *To provide reasons to support ideas (e.g The author persuades the reader by X.)* |

**Speaking:** *Supporting an Opinion*

# ELD Standards Record Sheet

**Teacher:** _____   **Class:** _____

**Standards:** *PI.C.11*                    **Guided Activities and Proficiency Levels:**

| Students: | #1 | #2 | #3 | #4 | #5 |
|---|---|---|---|---|---|
| | EM / EX / BR | EM / EX / BR | EM / EX / BR | EM / EX / BR | EM / EX / BR |
| | EM / EX / BR | EM / EX / BR | EM / EX / BR | EM / EX / BR | EM / EX / BR |
| | EM / EX / BR | EM / EX / BR | EM / EX / BR | EM / EX / BR | EM / EX / BR |
| | EM / EX / BR | EM / EX / BR | EM / EX / BR | EM / EX / BR | EM / EX / BR |
| | EM / EX / BR | EM / EX / BR | EM / EX / BR | EM / EX / BR | EM / EX / BR |
| | EM / EX / BR | EM / EX / BR | EM / EX / BR | EM / EX / BR | EM / EX / BR |
| | EM / EX / BR | EM / EX / BR | EM / EX / BR | EM / EX / BR | EM / EX / BR |
| | EM / EX / BR | EM / EX / BR | EM / EX / BR | EM / EX / BR | EM / EX / BR |
| | EM / EX / BR | EM / EX / BR | EM / EX / BR | EM / EX / BR | EM / EX / BR |
| | EM / EX / BR | EM / EX / BR | EM / EX / BR | EM / EX / BR | EM / EX / BR |
| | EM / EX / BR | EM / EX / BR | EM / EX / BR | EM / EX / BR | EM / EX / BR |
| | EM / EX / BR | EM / EX / BR | EM / EX / BR | EM / EX / BR | EM / EX / BR |
| | EM / EX / BR | EM / EX / BR | EM / EX / BR | EM / EX / BR | EM / EX / BR |
| | EM / EX / BR | EM / EX / BR | EM / EX / BR | EM / EX / BR | EM / EX / BR |
| | EM / EX / BR | EM / EX / BR | EM / EX / BR | EM / EX / BR | EM / EX / BR |
| | EM / EX / BR | EM / EX / BR | EM / EX / BR | EM / EX / BR | EM / EX / BR |
| | EM / EX / BR | EM / EX / BR | EM / EX / BR | EM / EX / BR | EM / EX / BR |
| | EM / EX / BR | EM / EX / BR | EM / EX / BR | EM / EX / BR | EM / EX / BR |
| | EM / EX / BR | EM / EX / BR | EM / EX / BR | EM / EX / BR | EM / EX / BR |

**Speaking:** *Supporting an Opinion*

# ELD Standards Record Sheet

Teacher: _____ Class: _____

Standards: *PII.B.3*

**Guided Activities and Proficiency Levels:**

| Students: | #1 | #2 | #3 | #4 | #5 |
|---|---|---|---|---|---|
| | EM / EX / BR | EM / EX / BR | EM / EX / BR | EM / EX / BR | EM / EX / BR |
| | EM / EX / BR | EM / EX / BR | EM / EX / BR | EM / EX / BR | EM / EX / BR |
| | EM / EX / BR | EM / EX / BR | EM / EX / BR | EM / EX / BR | EM / EX / BR |
| | EM / EX / BR | EM / EX / BR | EM / EX / BR | EM / EX / BR | EM / EX / BR |
| | EM / EX / BR | EM / EX / BR | EM / EX / BR | EM / EX / BR | EM / EX / BR |
| | EM / EX / BR | EM / EX / BR | EM / EX / BR | EM / EX / BR | EM / EX / BR |
| | EM / EX / BR | EM / EX / BR | EM / EX / BR | EM / EX / BR | EM / EX / BR |
| | EM / EX / BR | EM / EX / BR | EM / EX / BR | EM / EX / BR | EM / EX / BR |
| | EM / EX / BR | EM / EX / BR | EM / EX / BR | EM / EX / BR | EM / EX / BR |
| | EM / EX / BR | EM / EX / BR | EM / EX / BR | EM / EX / BR | EM / EX / BR |
| | EM / EX / BR | EM / EX / BR | EM / EX / BR | EM / EX / BR | EM / EX / BR |
| | EM / EX / BR | EM / EX / BR | EM / EX / BR | EM / EX / BR | EM / EX / BR |
| | EM / EX / BR | EM / EX / BR | EM / EX / BR | EM / EX / BR | EM / EX / BR |
| | EM / EX / BR | EM / EX / BR | EM / EX / BR | EM / EX / BR | EM / EX / BR |
| | EM / EX / BR | EM / EX / BR | EM / EX / BR | EM / EX / BR | EM / EX / BR |
| | EM / EX / BR | EM / EX / BR | EM / EX / BR | EM / EX / BR | EM / EX / BR |
| | EM / EX / BR | EM / EX / BR | EM / EX / BR | EM / EX / BR | EM / EX / BR |
| | EM / EX / BR | EM / EX / BR | EM / EX / BR | EM / EX / BR | EM / EX / BR |
| | EM / EX / BR | EM / EX / BR | EM / EX / BR | EM / EX / BR | EM / EX / BR |
| | EM / EX / BR | EM / EX / BR | EM / EX / BR | EM / EX / BR | EM / EX / BR |

**Speaking:** *Supporting an Opinion*

# ELD Standards Record Sheet

**Teacher:** _____ **Class:** _____

**Standards:** *PII.B.4*                    **Guided Activities and Proficiency Levels:**

| Students: | #1 | #2 | #3 | #4 | #5 |
|---|---|---|---|---|---|
| | EM / EX / BR | EM / EX / BR | EM / EX / BR | EM / EX / BR | EM / EX / BR |
| | EM / EX / BR | EM / EX / BR | EM / EX / BR | EM / EX / BR | EM / EX / BR |
| | EM / EX / BR | EM / EX / BR | EM / EX / BR | EM / EX / BR | EM / EX / BR |
| | EM / EX / BR | EM / EX / BR | EM / EX / BR | EM / EX / BR | EM / EX / BR |
| | EM / EX / BR | EM / EX / BR | EM / EX / BR | EM / EX / BR | EM / EX / BR |
| | EM / EX / BR | EM / EX / BR | EM / EX / BR | EM / EX / BR | EM / EX / BR |
| | EM / EX / BR | EM / EX / BR | EM / EX / BR | EM / EX / BR | EM / EX / BR |
| | EM / EX / BR | EM / EX / BR | EM / EX / BR | EM / EX / BR | EM / EX / BR |
| | EM / EX / BR | EM / EX / BR | EM / EX / BR | EM / EX / BR | EM / EX / BR |
| | EM / EX / BR | EM / EX / BR | EM / EX / BR | EM / EX / BR | EM / EX / BR |
| | EM / EX / BR | EM / EX / BR | EM / EX / BR | EM / EX / BR | EM / EX / BR |
| | EM / EX / BR | EM / EX / BR | EM / EX / BR | EM / EX / BR | EM / EX / BR |
| | EM / EX / BR | EM / EX / BR | EM / EX / BR | EM / EX / BR | EM / EX / BR |
| | EM / EX / BR | EM / EX / BR | EM / EX / BR | EM / EX / BR | EM / EX / BR |
| | EM / EX / BR | EM / EX / BR | EM / EX / BR | EM / EX / BR | EM / EX / BR |
| | EM / EX / BR | EM / EX / BR | EM / EX / BR | EM / EX / BR | EM / EX / BR |
| | EM / EX / BR | EM / EX / BR | EM / EX / BR | EM / EX / BR | EM / EX / BR |
| | EM / EX / BR | EM / EX / BR | EM / EX / BR | EM / EX / BR | EM / EX / BR |
| | EM / EX / BR | EM / EX / BR | EM / EX / BR | EM / EX / BR | EM / EX / BR |
| | EM / EX / BR | EM / EX / BR | EM / EX / BR | EM / EX / BR | EM / EX / BR |

# ELD Standards Record Sheet

**Teacher:** _____ **Class:** _____

**Standards**: *PII.B.5*

**Guided Activities and Proficiency Levels:**

| Students: | #1 | #2 | #3 | #4 | #5 |
|---|---|---|---|---|---|
| | EM / EX / BR | EM / EX / BR | EM / EX / BR | EM / EX / BR | EM / EX / BR |
| | EM / EX / BR | EM / EX / BR | EM / EX / BR | EM / EX / BR | EM / EX / BR |
| | EM / EX / BR | EM / EX / BR | EM / EX / BR | EM / EX / BR | EM / EX / BR |
| | EM / EX / BR | EM / EX / BR | EM / EX / BR | EM / EX / BR | EM / EX / BR |
| | EM / EX / BR | EM / EX / BR | EM / EX / BR | EM / EX / BR | EM / EX / BR |
| | EM / EX / BR | EM / EX / BR | EM / EX / BR | EM / EX / BR | EM / EX / BR |
| | EM / EX / BR | EM / EX / BR | EM / EX / BR | EM / EX / BR | EM / EX / BR |
| | EM / EX / BR | EM / EX / BR | EM / EX / BR | EM / EX / BR | EM / EX / BR |
| | EM / EX / BR | EM / EX / BR | EM / EX / BR | EM / EX / BR | EM / EX / BR |
| | EM / EX / BR | EM / EX / BR | EM / EX / BR | EM / EX / BR | EM / EX / BR |
| | EM / EX / BR | EM / EX / BR | EM / EX / BR | EM / EX / BR | EM / EX / BR |
| | EM / EX / BR | EM / EX / BR | EM / EX / BR | EM / EX / BR | EM / EX / BR |
| | EM / EX / BR | EM / EX / BR | EM / EX / BR | EM / EX / BR | EM / EX / BR |
| | EM / EX / BR | EM / EX / BR | EM / EX / BR | EM / EX / BR | EM / EX / BR |
| | EM / EX / BR | EM / EX / BR | EM / EX / BR | EM / EX / BR | EM / EX / BR |
| | EM / EX / BR | EM / EX / BR | EM / EX / BR | EM / EX / BR | EM / EX / BR |
| | EM / EX / BR | EM / EX / BR | EM / EX / BR | EM / EX / BR | EM / EX / BR |
| | EM / EX / BR | EM / EX / BR | EM / EX / BR | EM / EX / BR | EM / EX / BR |
| | EM / EX / BR | EM / EX / BR | EM / EX / BR | EM / EX / BR | EM / EX / BR |

**Speaking:** *Supporting an Opinion*

# ELD Standards Record Sheet

**Teacher:** _____ **Class:** _____

**Standards:** *PII.C.6*

**Guided Activities and Proficiency Levels:**

| Students: | #1 | #2 | #3 | #4 | #5 |
|---|---|---|---|---|---|
| | EM / EX / BR | EM / EX / BR | EM / EX / BR | EM / EX / BR | EM / EX / BR |
| | EM / EX / BR | EM / EX / BR | EM / EX / BR | EM / EX / BR | EM / EX / BR |
| | EM / EX / BR | EM / EX / BR | EM / EX / BR | EM / EX / BR | EM / EX / BR |
| | EM / EX / BR | EM / EX / BR | EM / EX / BR | EM / EX / BR | EM / EX / BR |
| | EM / EX / BR | EM / EX / BR | EM / EX / BR | EM / EX / BR | EM / EX / BR |
| | EM / EX / BR | EM / EX / BR | EM / EX / BR | EM / EX / BR | EM / EX / BR |
| | EM / EX / BR | EM / EX / BR | EM / EX / BR | EM / EX / BR | EM / EX / BR |
| | EM / EX / BR | EM / EX / BR | EM / EX / BR | EM / EX / BR | EM / EX / BR |
| | EM / EX / BR | EM / EX / BR | EM / EX / BR | EM / EX / BR | EM / EX / BR |
| | EM / EX / BR | EM / EX / BR | EM / EX / BR | EM / EX / BR | EM / EX / BR |
| | EM / EX / BR | EM / EX / BR | EM / EX / BR | EM / EX / BR | EM / EX / BR |
| | EM / EX / BR | EM / EX / BR | EM / EX / BR | EM / EX / BR | EM / EX / BR |
| | EM / EX / BR | EM / EX / BR | EM / EX / BR | EM / EX / BR | EM / EX / BR |
| | EM / EX / BR | EM / EX / BR | EM / EX / BR | EM / EX / BR | EM / EX / BR |
| | EM / EX / BR | EM / EX / BR | EM / EX / BR | EM / EX / BR | EM / EX / BR |
| | EM / EX / BR | EM / EX / BR | EM / EX / BR | EM / EX / BR | EM / EX / BR |
| | EM / EX / BR | EM / EX / BR | EM / EX / BR | EM / EX / BR | EM / EX / BR |
| | EM / EX / BR | EM / EX / BR | EM / EX / BR | EM / EX / BR | EM / EX / BR |
| | EM / EX / BR | EM / EX / BR | EM / EX / BR | EM / EX / BR | EM / EX / BR |

# Practice Activities

-------------------------------------------------------------

It is crucial to guide students in having **Constructive Conversations** utilizing skills and strategies that help them develop into productive thinkers and speakers.

- Help students **formulate** their ideas and thinking.
- Help students **explain and extend** their thinking so that it's clear and concise.
- Help students **support** their ideas and thinking with relevant support and information (i.e. from the picture).
- Help students **engage** in constructive dialogue with others through understanding, listening, and **consensus**.

-------------------------------------------------------------

**Practice Activities Direction:**

1.Students can work with partners, small group, or with an adult.

2.Students take turns using the Constructive Conversations script to help guide them through discussions about their opinions.

3.Students follow turn-taking protocols and use the Constructive Conversations script to build their oral language.

**Speaker #1**'s script is indicated by      **S1**

**Speaker #2**'s script is indicated by       **S2**

# Practice Activity #1

**Directions:** Practice having a constructive conversation about your opinion:

☐ With a partner    ☐ In a small group    ☐ With an adult

**S1** *I'm going to ask you for your opinion. You are learning about butterflies in science class. Would it be better to read a book about butterflies or watch a video about butterflies?*

**S2** *In my opinion, it would be better to...........*

**S1** *Can you explain your choice with relevant reasons?*

**S2** *In other words, one reason is.... What is your opinion?*

**S1** *In my opinion, it would be better to........*

**S2** *Can you explain your choice with relevant reasons?*

**S1** *In other words, one reason is.... Would you agree or disagree?*

**S2** *I would agree/disagree because...*

# Practice Activity #2

**Directions:** Practice having a constructive conversation about your opinion:

[ ] With a partner    [ ] In a small group    [ ] With an adult

**S1**   *I'm going to ask you for your opinion. You are learning about different animal biomes. Would it be better to do a research project about an ocean biome or a rainforest biome?*

**S2**   *In my opinion, it would be better to............*

**S1**   *Can you explain your choice with relevant reasons?*

**S2**   *In other words, one reason is.... What is your opinion?*

**S1**   *In my opinion, it would be better to........*

**S2**   *Can you explain your choice with relevant reasons?*

**S1**   *In other words, one reason is.... Would you agree or disagree?*

**S2**   *I would agree/disagree because...*

# Practice Activity #3

**Directions:** Practice having a constructive conversation about your opinion:

☐ With a partner     ☐ In a small group     ☐ With an adult

**S1**   *I'm going to ask you for your opinion. You class is working on an art project. Would it be better to work with a partner or by yourself on the art project?*

**S2**   *In my opinion, it would be better to...........*

**S1**   *Can you explain your choice with relevant reasons?*

**S2**   *In other words, one reason is.... What is your opinion?*

**S1**   *In my opinion, it would be better to.........*

**S2**   *Can you explain your choice with relevant reasons?*

**S1**   *In other words, one reason is.... Would you agree or disagree?*

**S2**   *I would agree/disagree because...*

# Practice Activity #4

**Directions:** Practice having a constructive conversation about your opinion:

☐ With a partner  ☐ In a small group  ☐ With an adult

**S1** *I'm going to ask you for your opinion. You class will have reading time after lunch. Would it be better to have the teacher read a book about sports or the solar system?*

**S2** *In my opinion, it would be better to............*

**S1** *Can you explain your choice with relevant reasons?*

**S2** *In other words, one reason is.... What is your opinion?*

**S1** *In my opinion, it would be better to.........*

**S2** *Can you explain your choice with relevant reasons?*

**S1** *In other words, one reason is.... Would you agree or disagree?*

**S2** *I would agree/disagree because...*

# Practice Activity #5

**Directions:** Practice having a constructive conversation about your opinion:

☐ With a partner  ☐ In a small group  ☐ With an adult

2.4 x 3.5

START

**S1** *I'm going to ask you for your opinion. You teacher gave your class free time during the math lesson. Would it be better to play a math game on the computer or play a math board game?*

**S2** *In my opinion, it would be better to...........*

**S1** *Can you explain your choice with relevant reasons?*

**S2** *In other words, one reason is.... What is your opinion?*

**S1** *In my opinion, it would be better to........*

**S2** *Can you explain your choice with relevant reasons?*

**S1** *In other words, one reason is.... Would you agree or disagree?*

**S2** *I would agree/disagree because...*

# Speaking
## *Retell a Narrative*

**This section includes:**
- Guided Activities
- Teacher's ELD Standards Record Sheet
- Student Practice Activities:
  - Constructive Conversations Guide
  - Narrative Retell Student Practice

- - - - - - - - - - - - - - - - - - - - - - - - - - - - - - - - - - - - - - - - -

## Alignment to CA ELD Standards:

| | Alignment to CCSS: |
|---|---|
| **Part I: Interacting in Meaningful Ways**<br>B.5 Listening Actively<br>Listening actively to spoken English in a range of social and academic contexts | SL.3.1–3; L.3.3<br>SL.4.1–3; L.4.3<br>SL.5.1–3; L.5.3 |
| **Part I: Interacting in Meaningful Ways**<br>C.9 Presenting<br>Expressing information and ideas in formal oral presentations on academic topics | SL.3.4–6; L.3.1, 3, 6<br>SL.4.4–6; L.4.1, 3, 6<br>SL.5.4–6; L.5.1, 3, 6 |
| **Part I: Interacting in Meaningful Ways**<br>C.12 Selecting Language Resources<br>Selecting and applying varied and precise vocabulary and language structures to effectively convey ideas | W.3.4–5; SL.3.4, 6; L.3.1, 3, 5–6<br>W.4.4–5; SL.4.4, 6; L.4.1, 3, 5–6<br>W.5.4–5; SL.5.4, 6; L.5.1, 3, 5–6 |
| **Part II: Learning About How English Works**<br>A.1 Structuring Cohesive Texts<br>Understanding text structure | RL.3.5; RI.3.5; W.3.1–5; SL.3.4<br>RL.4.5; RI.4.5; W.4.1–5; SL.4.4<br>RL.5.5; RI.5.5; W.5.1–5; SL.5.4 |
| **Part II: Learning About How English Works**<br>A.2 Structuring Cohesive Texts<br>Understanding Cohesion | RL.3.5; RI.3.5; W.3.1–4; SL.3.4; L.3.1, 3<br>RL.4.5; RI.4.5; W.4.1–4; SL.4.4; L.4.1, 3<br>RL.5.5; RI.5.5; W.5.1–4; SL.5.4; L.5.1, 3 |

- - - - - - - - - - - - - - - - - - - - - - - - - - - - - - - - - - - - - - - - -

# Speaking
## *Retell a Narrative*

- - - - - - - - - - - - - - - - - - - - - - - - - - - - - - - - - - - - -

**Alignment to CA ELD Standards:**      **Alignment to CCSS:**

**Part II: Learning About How English Works**

    B.3 Expanding & Enriching Ideas

    Using verbs and verb phrases

W.3.5; SL.3.6; L.3.1, 3, 6

W.4.5; SL.4.6; L.4.1, 3, 6

W.5.5; SL.5.6; L.5.1, 3, 6

**Part II: Learning About How English Works**

    B.4 Expanding & Enriching Ideas

    Using nouns and noun phrases

W.3.5; SL.3.6; L.3.1, 3, 6

W.4.5; SL.4.6; L.4.1, 3, 6

W.5.5; SL.5.6; L.5.1, 3, 6

**Part II: Learning About How English Works**

    B.5 Expanding & Enriching Ideas

    Modifying to add details

W.3.5; SL.3.4, 6; L.3.1, 3, 6

W.4.5; SL.4.4, 6; L.4.1, 3, 6

W.5.5; SL.5.4, 6; L.5.1, 3, 6

**Part II: Learning About How English Works**

    C.6 Expanding & Enriching Ideas

    Connecting Ideas

W.3.1–3, 5; SL.3.4, 6; L.3.1, 3, 6

W.4.1–3, 5; SL.4.4, 6; L.4.1, 3, 6

W.5.1–3, 5; SL.5.4, 6; L.5.1, 3, 6

- - - - - - - - - - - - - - - - - - - - - - - - - - - - - - - - - - - - -

## Guided Activities Direction:

1. Show students the series of pictures for the narrative.
2. Follow the teacher directions.
3. **Say** the **Teacher Script** (indicated by SAY )
4. Guide students through:
   - Actively listening to the narrative
   - Responding with a clear and detailed retelling of the narrative as supported by the pictures
   - Providing cohesive and connected ideas
   - Grammar and word choice are varied and effective
   - Responding in English with minimal grammatical errors
5. Then have students practice with additional retelling activities.

# Guided Activity #1

# Guided Activity #1

 **SAY**

Show the student the pictures for the narrative. Point to each one as you say the following.

**Look at the pictures. I am going to tell you a story about the pictures. Be sure to listen carefully. You will only hear the story ONCE. When I'm finished, you will use the pictures to tell the story back to me.**

 **SAY**

Point to the first picture of the narrative.

| 1 |

**David and his dad wanted to go to the zoo. They bought their entry tickets at the ticket booth. David was excited because he loved learning about animals.**

 **SAY**

Point to the second picture of the narrative.

| 2 |

**Once in the zoo, David and his dad went to see the giraffes. They were able to go to an upper deck to see the giraffes feeding on the tall trees. David enjoyed seeing the tall giraffes.**

 **SAY**

Point to the third picture of the narrative.

| 3 |

**Next, David and his dad went to see the elephants. They purchased some peanuts from the zoo keeper's booth for a quarter. David felt nervous at first, but had so much fun feeding the elephant.**

 **SAY**

Point to the fourth picture of the narrative.

| 4 |

**Before leaving, they stopped by the souvenir shop. David's dad bought him a hat that had a turtle on it. David loved his new hat. He thanked his dad for a wonderful day at the zoo.**

 **SAY**

**Now, using ALL of the pictures, tell the story back to me.**

# Guided Activity #2

# Guided Activity #2

· · · · · · · · · · · · · · · · · · · · · · · · · · · · · · · · · · · · · · · · · · · · · · · ·

**SAY**

Show the student the pictures for the narrative. Point to each one as you say the following.

**Look at the pictures. I am going to tell you a story about the pictures. Be sure to listen carefully. You will only hear the story ONCE. When I'm finished, you will use the pictures to tell the story back to me.**

**SAY**

Point to the first picture of the narrative.

**1**

**Tom wanted to build a new feeder for the squirrels in the backyard. He asked his mom to help him. They went to the garage and gathered a pile of wooden boards and some tools.**

**SAY**

Point to the second picture of the narrative.

**2**

**While his mom held the boards together tightly, Tom carefully hammered the nails into the boards. They made a small square shaped feeder.**

**SAY**

Point to the third picture of the narrative.

**3**

**Afterwards, Tom and his mom used paint and brushes to finish the feeder. They decorated it with green, blue, and yellow.**

**SAY**

Point to the fourth picture of the narrative.

**4**

**Tom's mom then placed the feeder in a tree in the backyard. Tom happily watched as a small squirrel approached the feeder cautiously. After a while, the little squirrel enjoyed the nuts that Tom had left in the feeder. Tom felt happy.**

**SAY**

**Now, using ALL of the pictures, tell the story back to me.**

# Guided Activity #3

**Speaking:** *Retell a Narrative*

# Guided Activity #3

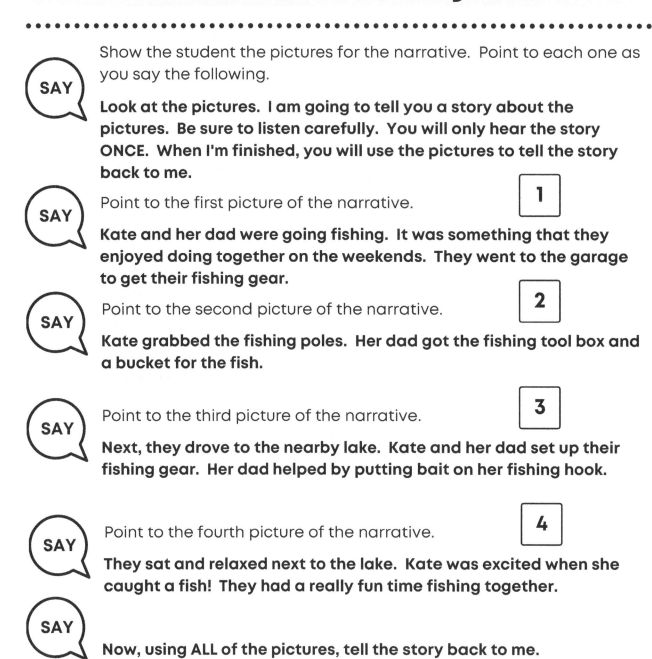

**SAY** Show the student the pictures for the narrative. Point to each one as you say the following.

**Look at the pictures. I am going to tell you a story about the pictures. Be sure to listen carefully. You will only hear the story ONCE. When I'm finished, you will use the pictures to tell the story back to me.**

**SAY** Point to the first picture of the narrative.

1

**Kate and her dad were going fishing. It was something that they enjoyed doing together on the weekends. They went to the garage to get their fishing gear.**

**SAY** Point to the second picture of the narrative.

2

**Kate grabbed the fishing poles. Her dad got the fishing tool box and a bucket for the fish.**

**SAY** Point to the third picture of the narrative.

3

**Next, they drove to the nearby lake. Kate and her dad set up their fishing gear. Her dad helped by putting bait on her fishing hook.**

**SAY** Point to the fourth picture of the narrative.

4

**They sat and relaxed next to the lake. Kate was excited when she caught a fish! They had a really fun time fishing together.**

**SAY** Now, using ALL of the pictures, tell the story back to me.

# Guided Activity #4

# Guided Activity #4

· · · · · · · · · · · · · · · · · · · · · · · · · · · · · · · · · · · · · · · · · · ·

**SAY** Show the student the pictures for the narrative. Point to each one as you say the following.

**Look at the pictures. I am going to tell you a story about the pictures. Be sure to listen carefully. You will only hear the story ONCE. When I'm finished, you will use the pictures to tell the story back to me.**

**SAY** Point to the first picture of the narrative.

1

**Blake's class is learning about volcanoes. She is going to build a model of a volcano. First, she gathers all the materials and supplies that she will need for her project.**

**SAY** Point to the second picture of the narrative.

2

**Next, Blake makes the volcano out of clay. She molds the volcano into a peak shape and places it on the cardboard base.**

**SAY** Point to the third picture of the narrative.

3

**Then Blake paints and decorates the volcano. She uses red paint to represent the lava flowing down the side. She makes little paper trees to put at the base of the volcano.**

**SAY** Point to the fourth picture of the narrative.

4

**Finally, Blake presents her volcano project to her teacher. Her teacher loves it and tells Blake that she did a wonderful job!**

**SAY**

**Now, using ALL of the pictures, tell the story back to me.**

# Guided Activity #5

# Guided Activity #5

**SAY** Show the student the pictures for the narrative. Point to each one as you say the following.

**Look at the pictures. I am going to tell you a story about the pictures. Be sure to listen carefully. You will only hear the story ONCE. When I'm finished, you will use the pictures to tell the story back to me.**

**SAY** Point to the first picture of the narrative.

1

**One weekend, Lisa and her family went to the lake. They packed their swim suits and a picnic basket full of food. Lisa was excited!**

**SAY** Point to the second picture of the narrative.

2

**At the lake, Lisa went swimming with her family. They had fun splashing around in the cool water. Lisa could swim for hours.**

**SAY** Point to the third picture of the narrative.

3

**Then Lisa and her family sat in the small canoe that they had brought along. They sat and fished for some time. It was very relaxing.**

**SAY** Point to the fourth picture of the narrative.

4

**After they went swimming, Lisa and her family sat under a big tree to enjoy their picnic basket full of food. Lisa ate a sandwich and an apple. It was a fun weekend at the lake!**

**SAY** 

**Now, using ALL of the pictures, tell the story back to me.**

# ELD Standards Record Sheet

<u>Directions:</u>

1. Look at the CA ELD standards (**BELOW**) that correspond to this section.
2. Reference these specific standards for the template Record Sheet.
3. Use the following template Record Sheet to monitor students' proficiency levels for the **GUIDED ACTIVITIES** in this section.
4. Fill out all the information. Circle, check, highlight the proficiency level. (*There is space for 20 students. Make additional copies, as needed*)
5. Retain for your records to be used during grading, parent/student conferences, lesson planning, ELD documentation, etc.

 **Suggestion: You can make one copy of each guided activity and/or the student practice sheets and laminate them. Organize the laminated sheets onto a book ring. Now it'll be easily accessible for whole group, small group, one-on-one, centers, etc. Copy as many of the ELD Standards Record Sheet as you need and keep it handy along with the activities**.

# ELD Standards Record Sheet

## CA ELD Standards & Proficiency Levels

### Part I: Interacting in Meaningful Ways
### *B.5 Listening Actively*

| EMERGING (EM) | EXPANDING (EX) | BRIDGING (BR) |
|---|---|---|
| Requires **Substantial** Support | Requires **Moderate** Support | Requires **Light** Support |
| **GRADE 3** | | |
| • Demonstrates active listening to:<br>  ◦ Read-alouds<br>  ◦ Oral presentations<br>• Ask/answer basic questions<br>• Uses support of oral sentence frames<br>• Requires substantial prompting and support | • Demonstrates active listening to:<br>  ◦ Read-alouds<br>  ◦ Oral presentations<br>• Ask/answer <u>detailed</u> questions<br>• Uses support of oral sentence frames<br>• Requires <u>occasional</u> prompting and moderate support | • Demonstrates active listening to:<br>  ◦ Read-alouds<br>  ◦ Oral presentations<br>• Ask/answer detailed questions<br>• Requires <u>minimal</u> prompting and light support |
| **GRADE 4** | | |
| • Demonstrates active listening to:<br>  ◦ Read-alouds<br>  ◦ Oral presentations<br>• Ask/answer basic questions<br>• Requires substantial prompting and support | • Demonstrates active listening to:<br>  ◦ Read-alouds<br>  ◦ Oral presentations<br>• Ask/answer <u>detailed</u> questions<br>• Requires <u>occasional</u> prompting and moderate support | • Demonstrates active listening to:<br>  ◦ Read-alouds<br>  ◦ Oral presentations<br>• Ask/answer detailed questions<br>• Requires <u>minimal</u> prompting and light support |
| **GRADE 5** | | |
| • Demonstrates active listening to:<br>  ◦ Read-alouds<br>  ◦ Oral presentations<br>• Ask/answer basic questions<br>• Requires substantial prompting and support | • Demonstrates active listening to:<br>  ◦ Read-alouds<br>  ◦ Oral presentations<br>• Ask/answer <u>detailed</u> questions<br>• Requires <u>occasional</u> prompting and moderate support | • Demonstrates active listening to:<br>  ◦ Read-alouds<br>  ◦ Oral presentations<br>• Ask/answer detailed questions<br>• Requires <u>minimal</u> prompting and light support |

# ELD Standards Record Sheet

## CA ELD Standards & Proficiency Levels:
### Part I: Interacting in Meaningful Ways
### *C.9 Presenting*

| EMERGING (EM) | EXPANDING (EX) | BRIDGING (BR) |
|---|---|---|
| *Requires **Substantial** Support* | *Requires **Moderate** Support* | *Requires **Light** Support* |
| **GRADE 3** | | |
| • *Plan and deliver very brief oral presentations (e.g. retelling a story, describing an animal)*<br>• *Produce basic statements to communicate basic information* | • *Plan and deliver <u>brief</u> oral presentations on a <u>variety of topics</u> (e.g. retelling a story, explaining a science process, etc.)* | • *Plan and deliver <u>longer</u> oral presentations on a variety of topics in a <u>variety of content areas</u> (e.g. retelling a story, explaining a science process or historical event, etc.)* |
| **GRADE 4** | | |
| • *Plan and deliver brief oral presentations on a variety of topics in a variety of content areas: (e.g. retelling a story, explaining a science process, reporting on a current event, recounting a memorable experience, etc.)*<br>• *Requires substantial support* | • *Plan and deliver <u>longer</u> oral presentations on a variety of topics and content areas: (e.g. retelling a story, explaining a science process, reporting on a current event, recounting a memorable experience, etc.)*<br>• *Requires <u>moderate</u> support* | • *Plan and deliver oral presentations on a variety of topics in a variety of content areas:(e.g. retelling a story, explaining a science process, reporting on a current event, recounting a memorable experience, etc.)*<br>• *Requires <u>light</u> support* |
| **GRADE 5** | | |
| • *Plan and deliver brief oral presentations on a variety of topics and content areas: (e.g. providing a report on a current event, reciting a poem, recounting an experience, explaining a science process)*<br>• *Requires moderate support (e.g. graphic organizers)* | • *Plan and deliver <u>longer</u> oral presentations on a variety of topics and content areas: (e.g. providing an opinion speech on a current event, reciting a poem, recounting an experience, explaining a science process)*<br>• *Requires <u>moderate</u> support* | • *Plan and deliver oral presentations on a variety of topics in a variety of content areas: (e.g. providing an opinion speech on a current event, reciting a poem, recounting an experience, explaining a science process)*<br>• *Requires <u>light</u> support* |

# ELD Standards Record Sheet

## CA ELD Standards & Proficiency Levels:
### Part I: Interacting in Meaningful Ways
### *C.12 Selecting Language Resources*

| EMERGING (EM) | EXPANDING (EX) | BRIDGING (BR) |
|---|---|---|
| *Requires **Substantial** Support* | *Requires **Moderate** Support* | *Requires **Light** Support* |
| **GRADE 3** | | |
| • *Use a select number of general academic and domain-specific words:*<br>　○ *to add detail (e.g. adding the word dangerous to describe a place, using the word habitat when describing animal behavior)*<br>• *Uses the words while speaking and writing* | • *Use a growing number of general academic and domain-specific words in order to:*<br>　○ *add detail*<br>　○ *create an effect (e.g. using the word suddenly to signal a change)*<br>　○ *create shades of meaning (e.g.scurry vs. dash)*<br>• *Uses the words while speaking and writing* | • *Use a wide variety of general academic and domain-specific words , synonyms, antonyms, and non-literal language to:*<br>　○ *create an effect*<br>　○ *precision*<br>　○ *shades of meaning*<br>• *Uses the words while speaking and writing* |
| **GRADE 4** | | |
| • *Use a select number of general academic and domain-specific words to create precision while speaking and writing*<br>• *Select a few frequently used affixes for accuracy and precision (e.g. She walks, I'm unhappy.)* | • *Use a growing number of general academic and domain-specific words, synonyms, and antonyms to create precision and shades of meaning while speaking and writing*<br>• *Select a growing number of frequently used affixes for accuracy and precision (e.g. She walked. He likes…, I'm unhappy.)* | • *Use a wide variety number of general academic and domain-specific words, synonyms, and antonyms, and figurative language to create precision and shades of meaning while speaking and writing*<br>• *Select a variety of appropriate affixes for accuracy and precision (e.g. She walking. I'm uncomfortable. They left reluctantly.)* |
| **GRADE 5** | | |
| • *Use a select number of general academic and domain-specific words to create precision while speaking and writing*<br>• *Select a few frequently used affixes for accuracy and precision (e.g. She walks, I'm unhappy.)* | • *Use a growing number of general academic and domain-specific words, synonyms, and antonyms to create precision and shades of meaning while speaking and writing*<br>• *Select a growing number of frequently used affixes for accuracy and precision (e.g. She walked. He likes…, I'm unhappy.)* | • *Use a wide variety number of general academic and domain-specific words, synonyms, and antonyms, and figurative language to create precision and shades of meaning while speaking and writing*<br>• *Select a variety of appropriate affixes for accuracy and precision (e.g. She walking. I'm uncomfortable. They left reluctantly.)* |

# ELD Standards Record Sheet

## CA ELD Standards & Proficiency Levels:
### Part II: Learning About How English Works
### A.1 Understanding Text Structure

| EMERGING (EM) | EXPANDING (EX) | BRIDGING (BR) |
|---|---|---|
| Requires **Substantial** Support | Requires **Moderate** Support | Requires **Light** Support |
| **GRADE 3** | | |
| • Apply understanding of how text types are organized to express ideas (e.g. how a story is organized sequentially)<br>• Comprehend & compose basic texts | • Apply understanding of how different text types are organized to express ideas (e.g. how a story is organized sequentially with predictable stages)<br>• Comprehend & write texts (w/ increasing cohesion) | • Apply understanding of how different text types are organized to express ideas (e.g. how a story is organized sequentially with predictable stages versus how opinion/arguments are structured logically, grouping related ideas)<br>• Comprehend & write cohesive texts |
| **GRADE 4** | | |
| • Apply understanding of how different text types are organized to express ideas (e.g. how a narrative is organized sequentially)<br>• Comprehend & compose basic texts | • Apply increasing understanding of how different text types are organized to express ideas (e.g. how a narrative is organized sequentially with predictable stages vs how an explanation is organized around ideas)<br>• Comprehend & write texts (w/ increasing cohesion) | • Apply understanding of how different text types are organized to express ideas (e.g. how a narrative is organized sequentially with predictable stages versus how opinion/arguments are structured logically, grouping related ideas)<br>• Comprehend & write cohesive texts |
| **GRADE 5** | | |
| • Apply basic understanding of how different text types are organized to express ideas (e.g. how a narrative is organized sequentially with predictable stages vs how opinions/ arguments are organized around ideas)<br>• Comprehend & compose basic texts | • Apply growing understanding of how different text types are organized to express ideas (e.g. how a narrative is organized sequentially with predictable stages vs how opinions/ arguments are structured logically around reasons and evidence)<br>• Comprehend & write texts (w/ increasing cohesion) | • Apply increasing understanding of how different text types are organized to express ideas (e.g. how a historical account is organized chronologically vs how opinions/arguments are structured logically around reasons and evidence)<br>• Comprehend & write cohesive texts |

# ELD Standards Record Sheet
## CA ELD Standards & Proficiency Levels
### Part II: Learning About How English Works
### *A.2 Understanding Cohesion*

| EMERGING (EM) | EXPANDING (EX) | BRIDGING (BR) |
|---|---|---|
| Requires **Substantial** Support | Requires **Moderate** Support | Requires **Light** Support |
| | **GRADE 3** | • Apply <u>increasing</u> understanding of language resources that refer the reader back or forward in text |
| • Apply basic understanding of language resources that refer the reader back or forward in text (e.g. how pronouns refer back to nouns in text) | • Apply <u>growing</u> understanding of language resources that refer the reader back or forward in text (e.g. how pronouns refer back to nouns in text) | • (e.g. how pronouns or synonyms refer back to nouns in text) |
| • Apply basic understanding of how ideas, events, or reasons are linked throughout a text using every day connecting words or phrases (e.g. then, next) | • Apply <u>growing</u> understanding of how ideas, events, or reasons are linked throughout a text using a <u>variety of</u> connecting words or phrases (e.g. at the beginning/end, first/next) | • Apply <u>increasing</u> understanding of how ideas, events, or reasons are linked throughout a text using an <u>increasing</u> variety of connecting and <u>transitional words</u> or phrases (e.g. for example, afterward, first/next/last) |
| • Comprehend & write basic texts | • Comprehend & write texts w/ <u>increasing</u> cohesion | • Comprehend & write cohesive texts |
| | **GRADE 4** | • Apply <u>increasing</u> understanding of language resources for referring the reader back or forward in text |
| • Apply basic understanding of language resources that refer the reader back or forward in text | • Apply <u>growing</u> understanding of language resources for referring the reader back or forward in text (e.g. how pronouns or synonyms refer back to nouns in text) | • (e.g. how pronouns, synonyms, or nominalizations refer back to nouns in text) |
| • (e.g. how pronouns refer back to nouns in text) | | |
| • Apply basic understanding of how ideas, events, or reasons are linked throughout a text using every day connecting words or phrases (e.g. first, yesterday) | • Apply <u>growing</u> understanding of how ideas, events, or reasons are linked throughout a text using a <u>variety</u> of connecting words or phrases(e.g. since, next, for example) | • Apply <u>increasing</u> understanding of how ideas, events, or reasons are linked throughout a text using an <u>increasing</u> variety of <u>academic</u> connecting and <u>transitional</u> words or phrases (e.g. for instance, in addition, at the end) |
| • Comprehend & write basic texts | • Comprehend & write texts w/ <u>increasing</u> cohesion | • Comprehend & write cohesive texts |
| | **GRADE 5** | • Apply <u>increasing</u> understanding of language resources for referring the reader back or forward in text (e.g. how pronouns, synonyms, or nominalizations refer back to nouns in text) |
| • Apply basic understanding of language resources for referring the reader back or forward in text | • Apply <u>growing</u> understanding of language resources for referring the reader back or forward in text (e.g. how pronouns or synonyms refer back to nouns in text) | |
| • (e.g. how pronouns refer back to nouns in text) | | |
| • Apply basic understanding of how ideas, events, or reasons are linked throughout a text using a select set of every day connecting words or phrases (e.g. first/next, at the beginning) | • Apply <u>growing</u> understanding of how ideas, events, or reasons are linked throughout a text using a <u>variety</u> of connecting words or phrases (e.g. for example, in the first place, as a result) | • Apply <u>increasing</u> understanding of how ideas, events, or reasons are linked throughout a text using an <u>increasing</u> variety of <u>academic</u> connecting and <u>transitional</u> words or phrases (e.g. consequently, specifically, however) |
| • Comprehend & write basic texts | • Comprehend & write texts w/ <u>increasing</u> cohesion | • Comprehend & write cohesive texts |

# ELD Standards Record Sheet

## CA ELD Standards & Proficiency Levels

**Part II:** Learning About How English Works
### B.3 Using Verbs and Verb Phrases

| EMERGING (EM)➤ | EXPANDING (EX) ➤ | BRIDGING (BR) |
|---|---|---|
| Requires **Substantial** Support | Requires **Moderate** Support | Requires **Light** Support |
| **GRADE 3** | | |
| • Use frequently used verbs<br>• Use different verb types (e.g. doing, saying, being/having, thinking/feeling)<br>• Use different verb tenses (e.g. simple past for recounting an experience)<br>• Appropriate for the text type and discipline to convey time | • Use a <u>growing number</u> of verb types (e.g. doing, saying, being/having, thinking/feeling)<br>• Use a <u>growing number</u> of verb tenses (e.g. simple past for retelling, simple present for a science description)<br>• Appropriate for the text type and discipline to convey time | • Use a <u>variety</u> of verb types (e.g. doing, saying, being/having, thinking/feeling)<br>• Use a <u>variety</u> of verb tenses (e.g. simple present for a science description, simple future to predict)<br>• Appropriate for the text type and discipline to convey time |
| **GRADE 4** | | • Use various verb |
| • Use various verbs<br>• Use various verb types (e.g. doing, saying, being/having, thinking/feeling)<br>• Use various verb tenses (e.g. simple past for recounting an experience)<br>• Appropriate for the text type and discipline for familiar topics | • Use various verbs<br>• Use various verb types (e.g. doing, saying, being/having, thinking/feeling)<br>• Use various verb tenses (e.g. simple past for retelling, timeless present for science explanation)<br>• Appropriate for the <u>task</u>, text type and discipline<br>• <u>For an increasing variety of familiar and new topics</u> | • Use various verb types (e.g. doing, saying, being/having, thinking/feeling)<br>• Use various verb tenses(e.g. timeless present for science explanation, mixture of past and present for historical information report)<br>• Appropriate for the task and text type<br>• For a <u>variety</u> of familiar and new topics |
| **GRADE 5** | | • Use various verb types (e.g. doing, saying, being/having, thinking/feeling) |
| • Use frequently used verbs (e.g. take, like, eat)<br>• Use various verb types (e.g. doing, saying, being/having, thinking/feeling)<br>• Use various verb tenses (e.g. simple past for recounting an experience)<br>• Appropriate for the text type and discipline for familiar topics | • Use <u>various</u> verb types (e.g. doing, saying, being/having, thinking/feeling)<br>• Use various verb tenses (e.g. simple past for retelling, timeless present for science a description)<br>• Appropriate for the <u>task</u>, text type and discipline<br>• <u>For an increasing variety of topics</u> | • Use various verb types (e.g. doing, saying, being/having, thinking/feeling)<br>• Use various verb tenses (e.g. timeless present for science description, mixture of past and present for narrative or history explanation)<br>• Appropriate for the task and text type<br>• For a <u>variety</u> of topics |

# ELD Standards Record Sheet

## CA ELD Standards & Proficiency Levels

**Part II:** Learning About How English Works
### B.4 Using Nouns and Noun Phrases

| EMERGING (EM) | EXPANDING (EX) | BRIDGING (BR) |
|---|---|---|
| Requires **Substantial** Support | Requires **Moderate** Support | Requires **Light** Support |
| | **GRADE 3** | |
| • Expand noun phrases in simple ways in order to enrich:<br>  ○ The meaning of sentences<br>  ○ Add details about ideas, people, things, etc. (e.g. adding an adjective to a noun) | • Expand noun phrases in a <u>growing number</u> of ways in order to enrich:<br>  ○ The meaning of sentences<br>  ○ Add details about ideas, people, things, etc. (e.g. adding comparative/superlative adjectives to nouns) | • Expand noun phrases in a <u>variety</u> of ways in order to enrich:<br>  ○ The meaning of sentences and<br>  ○ Add details about ideas, people, things, etc. (e.g. adding comparative/superlative adjectives to nouns, simple clause embedding) |
| | **GRADE 4** | |
| • Expand noun phrases in simple ways in order to enrich:<br>  ○ The meaning of sentences<br>  ○ Add details about ideas, people, things, etc. (e.g. adding an adjective) | • Expand noun phrases in a <u>variety</u> of ways in order to enrich:<br>  ○ The meaning of sentences<br>  ○ Add details about ideas, people, things, etc. (e.g. adding adjectives to noun phrases or simple clause embedding) | • Expand noun phrases in an <u>increasing variety</u> of ways in order to enrich:<br>  ○ The meaning of sentences and<br>  ○ Add details about ideas, people, things, etc. (e.g. adding general academic adjectives and adverbs to noun phrases or more complex clause embedding) |
| | **GRADE 5** | |
| • Expand noun phrases in simple ways in order to enrich:<br>  ○ The meaning of sentences<br>  ○ Add details about ideas, people, things, etc. (e.g. adding an adjective to a noun) | • Expand noun phrases in a <u>variety</u> of ways in order to enrich:<br>  ○ The meaning of sentences<br>  ○ Add details about ideas, people, things, etc. (e.g. adding comparative/superlative adjectives to noun phrases or simple clause embedding) | • Expand noun phrases in an <u>increasing variety</u> of ways in order to enrich:<br>  ○ The meaning of sentences<br>  ○ Add details about ideas, people, things, etc. (e.g. adding comparative/superlative and general academic adjectives to noun phrases or more complex clause embedding) |

# ELD Standards Record Sheet

## CA ELD Standards & Proficiency Levels

**Part II:** Learning About How English Works
### *B.5 Modifying to Add Details*

| EMERGING (EM) | EXPANDING (EX) | BRIDGING (BR) |
|---|---|---|
| Requires **Substantial** Support | Requires **Moderate** Support | Requires **Light** Support |
| **GRADE 3** | | |
| • *Expand sentences with adverbials (e.g. adverbs, adverb phrases, prepositional phrases)*<br>• *Use these to provide details about a familiar activity or process (e.g. time, manner, place, cause) (e.g. They walked to the soccer field.)* | • *Expand sentences with adverbials (e.g. adverbs, adverb phrases, prepositional phrases)*<br>• *Use these to provide details about a familiar or <u>new activity</u> or process (e.g. time, manner, place, cause) (e.g. They worked quietly; They ran across the soccer field.)* | • *Expand sentences with adverbials (e.g. adverbs, adverb phrases, prepositional phrases)*<br>• *Use these to provide details about a <u>range</u> of familiar and new activities or processes. (e.g. time, manner, place, cause) (e.g. They worked quietly all night in their room.)* |
| **GRADE 4** | | |
| • *Expand sentences with familiar adverbials (e.g. basic prepositional phrases)*<br>• *Use these to provide details about a familiar activity or process (e.g. time, manner, place, cause) (e.g. They walked to the soccer field.)* | • *Expand sentences with a <u>growing variety</u> of adverbials (e.g. adverbs, prepositional phrases)*<br>• *Use these to provide details about a familiar or <u>new activity</u> or process (e.g. time, manner, place, cause) (e.g. They worked quietly; They ran across the soccer field.)* | • *Expand sentences with a <u>variety</u> of adverbials (e.g. adverbs, adverb phrases, prepositional phrases)*<br>• *Use these to provide details about a <u>variety</u> of familiar and new activities or processes.(e.g. time, manner, place, cause) (e.g. They worked quietly all night in their room.)* |
| **GRADE 5** | | |
| • *Expand and enrich sentences with adverbials (e.g. adverbs, adverb phrases, prepositional phrases)*<br>• *Use these to provide details about a familiar activity or process (e.g. time, manner, place, cause)* | • *Expand and enrich sentences with adverbials (e.g. adverbs, adverb phrases, prepositional phrases)*<br>• *Use these to provide details about a familiar or <u>new activity</u> or process (e.g. time, manner, place, cause)* | • *Expand and enrich sentences with adverbials (e.g. adverbs, adverb phrases, prepositional phrases)*<br>• *Use these to provide details about a <u>variety</u> of familiar and new activities or processes.(e.g. time, manner, place, cause)* |

# ELD Standards Record Sheet
## CA ELD Standards & Proficiency Levels
**Part II:** Learning About How English Works
### *C.6 Connecting Ideas*

| EMERGING (EM)→ | ➤ EXPANDING (EX) | ➤ BRIDGING (BR) |
|---|---|---|
| *Requires **Substantial** Support* | *Requires **Moderate** Support* | *Requires **Light** Support* |
| | **GRADE 3** | |
| • *Combine clauses in a few basic ways* <br> • *To make connections between and to join ideas (e.g. creating compound sentences using and, but, so)* | • *Combine clauses in an <u>increasing variety</u> of ways (e.g. creating compound and complex sentences)* <br> • *to make connections between and to join ideas, for example:* <br>   ◦ *<u>to express cause/effect (e.g. The deer ran because the mountain lion came.)</u>* <br>   ◦ *<u>to make a concession (e.g. She studied all night even though she wasn't feeling well.)</u>* | • *Combine clauses in a <u>wide variety</u> of ways (e.g. creating compound and complex sentences)* <br> • *to make connections between and to join ideas, for example:* <br>   ◦ *to express cause/effect (e.g. The deer ran because the mountain lion approached them.)* <br>   ◦ *to make a concession(e.g. She studied all night even though she wasn't feeling well.)* <br>   ◦ *<u>to link two ideas that happen at the same time (e.g. The cubs played while their mother hunted.)</u>* |
| | **GRADE 4** | |
| • *Combine clauses in a few basic ways* <br> • *To make connections between and to join ideas in sentences (e.g. creating compound sentences using coordinate conjunctions, such as and, but, so)* | • *Combine clauses in an <u>increasing variety</u> of ways (e.g. creating complex sentences using familiar subordinate conjunctions)* <br> • *to make connections between and to join ideas in sentences, for example:* <br>   ◦ *<u>to express cause/effect (e.g. The deer ran because the mountain lion came.)</u>* <br>   ◦ *<u>to make a concession (e.g. She studied all night even though she wasn't feeling well.)</u>* | • *Combine clauses in a <u>wide variety</u> of ways (e.g. creating complex sentences using a variety of subordinate conjunctions)* <br> • *to make connections between and to join ideas, for example:* <br>   ◦ *to express cause/effect (e.g. Since the lion was at the waterhole, the deer ran away.)* <br>   ◦ *to make a concession* <br>   ◦ *<u>to link two ideas that happen at the same time (e.g. The cubs played while their mother hunted.)</u>* |
| | **GRADE 5** | |
| • *Combine clauses in a few basic ways* <br> • *To make connections between and to join ideas* <br> • *To provide evidence to support ideas or opinions (e.g. You must X because X.)(e.g. creating compound sentences using and, but, so)* | • *Combine clauses in an <u>increasing variety</u> of ways (e.g. creating compound and complex sentences)* <br> • *to make connections between and to join ideas, for example:* <br>   ◦ *<u>to express cause/effect (e.g. The deer ran because the mountain lion came.)</u>* <br>   ◦ *<u>to make a concession(e.g. She studied all night even though she wasn't feeling well.)</u>* <br> • *To provide reasons to support ideas (e.g. X is an extremely good book because X)* | • *Combine clauses in a <u>wide variety</u> of ways (e.g. creating compound and complex sentences)* <br> • *to make connections between and to join ideas, for example:* <br>   ◦ *to express cause/effect (e.g. The deer ran because the mountain lion approached them.)* <br>   ◦ *to make a concession (e.g. She studied all night even though she wasn't feeling well.)* <br>   ◦ *<u>to link two ideas that happen at the same time (e.g. The cubs played while their mother hunted.)</u>* <br> • *To provide reasons to support ideas (e.g The author persuades the reader by X.)* |

**Speaking:** *Retell a Narrative*

# ELD Standards Record Sheet

**Teacher:** _____ **Class:** _____

**Standards:** *PI.B.5*

**Guided Activities and Proficiency Levels:**

| Students: | #1 | #2 | #3 | #4 | #5 |
|---|---|---|---|---|---|
| | EM / EX / BR | EM / EX / BR | EM / EX / BR | EM / EX / BR | EM / EX / BR |
| | EM / EX / BR | EM / EX / BR | EM / EX / BR | EM / EX / BR | EM / EX / BR |
| | EM / EX / BR | EM / EX / BR | EM / EX / BR | EM / EX / BR | EM / EX / BR |
| | EM / EX / BR | EM / EX / BR | EM / EX / BR | EM / EX / BR | EM / EX / BR |
| | EM / EX / BR | EM / EX / BR | EM / EX / BR | EM / EX / BR | EM / EX / BR |
| | EM / EX / BR | EM / EX / BR | EM / EX / BR | EM / EX / BR | EM / EX / BR |
| | EM / EX / BR | EM / EX / BR | EM / EX / BR | EM / EX / BR | EM / EX / BR |
| | EM / EX / BR | EM / EX / BR | EM / EX / BR | EM / EX / BR | EM / EX / BR |
| | EM / EX / BR | EM / EX / BR | EM / EX / BR | EM / EX / BR | EM / EX / BR |
| | EM / EX / BR | EM / EX / BR | EM / EX / BR | EM / EX / BR | EM / EX / BR |
| | EM / EX / BR | EM / EX / BR | EM / EX / BR | EM / EX / BR | EM / EX / BR |
| | EM / EX / BR | EM / EX / BR | EM / EX / BR | EM / EX / BR | EM / EX / BR |
| | EM / EX / BR | EM / EX / BR | EM / EX / BR | EM / EX / BR | EM / EX / BR |
| | EM / EX / BR | EM / EX / BR | EM / EX / BR | EM / EX / BR | EM / EX / BR |
| | EM / EX / BR | EM / EX / BR | EM / EX / BR | EM / EX / BR | EM / EX / BR |
| | EM / EX / BR | EM / EX / BR | EM / EX / BR | EM / EX / BR | EM / EX / BR |
| | EM / EX / BR | EM / EX / BR | EM / EX / BR | EM / EX / BR | EM / EX / BR |
| | EM / EX / BR | EM / EX / BR | EM / EX / BR | EM / EX / BR | EM / EX / BR |
| | EM / EX / BR | EM / EX / BR | EM / EX / BR | EM / EX / BR | EM / EX / BR |

# ELD Standards Record Sheet

**Teacher:** _____  **Class:** _____

**Standards:** *PI.C.9*

**Guided Activities and Proficiency Levels:**

| Students: | #1 | #2 | #3 | #4 | #5 |
|---|---|---|---|---|---|
| _____ | EM / EX / BR | EM / EX / BR | EM / EX / BR | EM / EX / BR | EM / EX / BR |
| _____ | EM / EX / BR | EM / EX / BR | EM / EX / BR | EM / EX / BR | EM / EX / BR |
| _____ | EM / EX / BR | EM / EX / BR | EM / EX / BR | EM / EX / BR | EM / EX / BR |
| _____ | EM / EX / BR | EM / EX / BR | EM / EX / BR | EM / EX / BR | EM / EX / BR |
| _____ | EM / EX / BR | EM / EX / BR | EM / EX / BR | EM / EX / BR | EM / EX / BR |
| _____ | EM / EX / BR | EM / EX / BR | EM / EX / BR | EM / EX / BR | EM / EX / BR |
| _____ | EM / EX / BR | EM / EX / BR | EM / EX / BR | EM / EX / BR | EM / EX / BR |
| _____ | EM / EX / BR | EM / EX / BR | EM / EX / BR | EM / EX / BR | EM / EX / BR |
| _____ | EM / EX / BR | EM / EX / BR | EM / EX / BR | EM / EX / BR | EM / EX / BR |
| _____ | EM / EX / BR | EM / EX / BR | EM / EX / BR | EM / EX / BR | EM / EX / BR |
| _____ | EM / EX / BR | EM / EX / BR | EM / EX / BR | EM / EX / BR | EM / EX / BR |
| _____ | EM / EX / BR | EM / EX / BR | EM / EX / BR | EM / EX / BR | EM / EX / BR |
| _____ | EM / EX / BR | EM / EX / BR | EM / EX / BR | EM / EX / BR | EM / EX / BR |
| _____ | EM / EX / BR | EM / EX / BR | EM / EX / BR | EM / EX / BR | EM / EX / BR |
| _____ | EM / EX / BR | EM / EX / BR | EM / EX / BR | EM / EX / BR | EM / EX / BR |
| _____ | EM / EX / BR | EM / EX / BR | EM / EX / BR | EM / EX / BR | EM / EX / BR |
| _____ | EM / EX / BR | EM / EX / BR | EM / EX / BR | EM / EX / BR | EM / EX / BR |
| _____ | EM / EX / BR | EM / EX / BR | EM / EX / BR | EM / EX / BR | EM / EX / BR |
| _____ | EM / EX / BR | EM / EX / BR | EM / EX / BR | EM / EX / BR | EM / EX / BR |
| _____ | EM / EX / BR | EM / EX / BR | EM / EX / BR | EM / EX / BR | EM / EX / BR |

**Speaking:** *Retell a Narrative*

# ELD Standards Record Sheet

**Teacher:** _____  **Class:** _____

**Standards**: *PI.C.12*

**Guided Activities and Proficiency Levels:**

| Students: | #1 | #2 | #3 | #4 | #5 |
|---|---|---|---|---|---|
| | EM / EX / BR | EM / EX / BR | EM / EX / BR | EM / EX / BR | EM / EX / BR |
| | EM / EX / BR | EM / EX / BR | EM / EX / BR | EM / EX / BR | EM / EX / BR |
| | EM / EX / BR | EM / EX / BR | EM / EX / BR | EM / EX / BR | EM / EX / BR |
| | EM / EX / BR | EM / EX / BR | EM / EX / BR | EM / EX / BR | EM / EX / BR |
| | EM / EX / BR | EM / EX / BR | EM / EX / BR | EM / EX / BR | EM / EX / BR |
| | EM / EX / BR | EM / EX / BR | EM / EX / BR | EM / EX / BR | EM / EX / BR |
| | EM / EX / BR | EM / EX / BR | EM / EX / BR | EM / EX / BR | EM / EX / BR |
| | EM / EX / BR | EM / EX / BR | EM / EX / BR | EM / EX / BR | EM / EX / BR |
| | EM / EX / BR | EM / EX / BR | EM / EX / BR | EM / EX / BR | EM / EX / BR |
| | EM / EX / BR | EM / EX / BR | EM / EX / BR | EM / EX / BR | EM / EX / BR |
| | EM / EX / BR | EM / EX / BR | EM / EX / BR | EM / EX / BR | EM / EX / BR |
| | EM / EX / BR | EM / EX / BR | EM / EX / BR | EM / EX / BR | EM / EX / BR |
| | EM / EX / BR | EM / EX / BR | EM / EX / BR | EM / EX / BR | EM / EX / BR |
| | EM / EX / BR | EM / EX / BR | EM / EX / BR | EM / EX / BR | EM / EX / BR |
| | EM / EX / BR | EM / EX / BR | EM / EX / BR | EM / EX / BR | EM / EX / BR |
| | EM / EX / BR | EM / EX / BR | EM / EX / BR | EM / EX / BR | EM / EX / BR |
| | EM / EX / BR | EM / EX / BR | EM / EX / BR | EM / EX / BR | EM / EX / BR |
| | EM / EX / BR | EM / EX / BR | EM / EX / BR | EM / EX / BR | EM / EX / BR |
| | EM / EX / BR | EM / EX / BR | EM / EX / BR | EM / EX / BR | EM / EX / BR |
| | EM / EX / BR | EM / EX / BR | EM / EX / BR | EM / EX / BR | EM / EX / BR |

**Speaking:** *Retell a Narrative*

# ELD Standards Record Sheet

**Teacher:** _____ **Class:** _____

**Standards:** *PII.A.1*  **Guided Activities and Proficiency Levels:**

| Students: | #1 | #2 | #3 | #4 | #5 |
|---|---|---|---|---|---|
| | EM / EX / BR | EM / EX / BR | EM / EX / BR | EM / EX / BR | EM / EX / BR |
| | EM / EX / BR | EM / EX / BR | EM / EX / BR | EM / EX / BR | EM / EX / BR |
| | EM / EX / BR | EM / EX / BR | EM / EX / BR | EM / EX / BR | EM / EX / BR |
| | EM / EX / BR | EM / EX / BR | EM / EX / BR | EM / EX / BR | EM / EX / BR |
| | EM / EX / BR | EM / EX / BR | EM / EX / BR | EM / EX / BR | EM / EX / BR |
| | EM / EX / BR | EM / EX / BR | EM / EX / BR | EM / EX / BR | EM / EX / BR |
| | EM / EX / BR | EM / EX / BR | EM / EX / BR | EM / EX / BR | EM / EX / BR |
| | EM / EX / BR | EM / EX / BR | EM / EX / BR | EM / EX / BR | EM / EX / BR |
| | EM / EX / BR | EM / EX / BR | EM / EX / BR | EM / EX / BR | EM / EX / BR |
| | EM / EX / BR | EM / EX / BR | EM / EX / BR | EM / EX / BR | EM / EX / BR |
| | EM / EX / BR | EM / EX / BR | EM / EX / BR | EM / EX / BR | EM / EX / BR |
| | EM / EX / BR | EM / EX / BR | EM / EX / BR | EM / EX / BR | EM / EX / BR |
| | EM / EX / BR | EM / EX / BR | EM / EX / BR | EM / EX / BR | EM / EX / BR |
| | EM / EX / BR | EM / EX / BR | EM / EX / BR | EM / EX / BR | EM / EX / BR |
| | EM / EX / BR | EM / EX / BR | EM / EX / BR | EM / EX / BR | EM / EX / BR |
| | EM / EX / BR | EM / EX / BR | EM / EX / BR | EM / EX / BR | EM / EX / BR |
| | EM / EX / BR | EM / EX / BR | EM / EX / BR | EM / EX / BR | EM / EX / BR |
| | EM / EX / BR | EM / EX / BR | EM / EX / BR | EM / EX / BR | EM / EX / BR |
| | EM / EX / BR | EM / EX / BR | EM / EX / BR | EM / EX / BR | EM / EX / BR |
| | EM / EX / BR | EM / EX / BR | EM / EX / BR | EM / EX / BR | EM / EX / BR |

**Speaking:** *Retell a Narrative*

# ELD Standards Record Sheet

**Teacher:** _____ **Class:** _____

**Standards**: *PII.A.2*          **Guided Activities and Proficiency Levels:**

| Students: | #1 | #2 | #3 | #4 | #5 |
|---|---|---|---|---|---|
| | EM / EX / BR | EM / EX / BR | EM / EX / BR | EM / EX / BR | EM / EX / BR |
| | EM / EX / BR | EM / EX / BR | EM / EX / BR | EM / EX / BR | EM / EX / BR |
| | EM / EX / BR | EM / EX / BR | EM / EX / BR | EM / EX / BR | EM / EX / BR |
| | EM / EX / BR | EM / EX / BR | EM / EX / BR | EM / EX / BR | EM / EX / BR |
| | EM / EX / BR | EM / EX / BR | EM / EX / BR | EM / EX / BR | EM / EX / BR |
| | EM / EX / BR | EM / EX / BR | EM / EX / BR | EM / EX / BR | EM / EX / BR |
| | EM / EX / BR | EM / EX / BR | EM / EX / BR | EM / EX / BR | EM / EX / BR |
| | EM / EX / BR | EM / EX / BR | EM / EX / BR | EM / EX / BR | EM / EX / BR |
| | EM / EX / BR | EM / EX / BR | EM / EX / BR | EM / EX / BR | EM / EX / BR |
| | EM / EX / BR | EM / EX / BR | EM / EX / BR | EM / EX / BR | EM / EX / BR |
| | EM / EX / BR | EM / EX / BR | EM / EX / BR | EM / EX / BR | EM / EX / BR |
| | EM / EX / BR | EM / EX / BR | EM / EX / BR | EM / EX / BR | EM / EX / BR |
| | EM / EX / BR | EM / EX / BR | EM / EX / BR | EM / EX / BR | EM / EX / BR |
| | EM / EX / BR | EM / EX / BR | EM / EX / BR | EM / EX / BR | EM / EX / BR |
| | EM / EX / BR | EM / EX / BR | EM / EX / BR | EM / EX / BR | EM / EX / BR |
| | EM / EX / BR | EM / EX / BR | EM / EX / BR | EM / EX / BR | EM / EX / BR |
| | EM / EX / BR | EM / EX / BR | EM / EX / BR | EM / EX / BR | EM / EX / BR |
| | EM / EX / BR | EM / EX / BR | EM / EX / BR | EM / EX / BR | EM / EX / BR |
| | EM / EX / BR | EM / EX / BR | EM / EX / BR | EM / EX / BR | EM / EX / BR |
| | EM / EX / BR | EM / EX / BR | EM / EX / BR | EM / EX / BR | EM / EX / BR |

**Speaking:** *Retell a Narrative*

# ELD Standards Record Sheet

**Teacher:** _____ **Class:** _____

**Standards:** *PII.B.3*

**Guided Activities and Proficiency Levels:**

| Students: | #1 | #2 | #3 | #4 | #5 |
|---|---|---|---|---|---|
| | EM / EX / BR | EM / EX / BR | EM / EX / BR | EM / EX / BR | EM / EX / BR |
| | EM / EX / BR | EM / EX / BR | EM / EX / BR | EM / EX / BR | EM / EX / BR |
| | EM / EX / BR | EM / EX / BR | EM / EX / BR | EM / EX / BR | EM / EX / BR |
| | EM / EX / BR | EM / EX / BR | EM / EX / BR | EM / EX / BR | EM / EX / BR |
| | EM / EX / BR | EM / EX / BR | EM / EX / BR | EM / EX / BR | EM / EX / BR |
| | EM / EX / BR | EM / EX / BR | EM / EX / BR | EM / EX / BR | EM / EX / BR |
| | EM / EX / BR | EM / EX / BR | EM / EX / BR | EM / EX / BR | EM / EX / BR |
| | EM / EX / BR | EM / EX / BR | EM / EX / BR | EM / EX / BR | EM / EX / BR |
| | EM / EX / BR | EM / EX / BR | EM / EX / BR | EM / EX / BR | EM / EX / BR |
| | EM / EX / BR | EM / EX / BR | EM / EX / BR | EM / EX / BR | EM / EX / BR |
| | EM / EX / BR | EM / EX / BR | EM / EX / BR | EM / EX / BR | EM / EX / BR |
| | EM / EX / BR | EM / EX / BR | EM / EX / BR | EM / EX / BR | EM / EX / BR |
| | EM / EX / BR | EM / EX / BR | EM / EX / BR | EM / EX / BR | EM / EX / BR |
| | EM / EX / BR | EM / EX / BR | EM / EX / BR | EM / EX / BR | EM / EX / BR |
| | EM / EX / BR | EM / EX / BR | EM / EX / BR | EM / EX / BR | EM / EX / BR |
| | EM / EX / BR | EM / EX / BR | EM / EX / BR | EM / EX / BR | EM / EX / BR |
| | EM / EX / BR | EM / EX / BR | EM / EX / BR | EM / EX / BR | EM / EX / BR |
| | EM / EX / BR | EM / EX / BR | EM / EX / BR | EM / EX / BR | EM / EX / BR |
| | EM / EX / BR | EM / EX / BR | EM / EX / BR | EM / EX / BR | EM / EX / BR |
| | EM / EX / BR | EM / EX / BR | EM / EX / BR | EM / EX / BR | EM / EX / BR |

# ELD Standards Record Sheet

**Teacher:** _____ **Class:** _____

**Standards:** *PII.B.4*

**Guided Activities and Proficiency Levels:**

| Students: | #1 | #2 | #3 | #4 | #5 |
|---|---|---|---|---|---|
| | EM / EX / BR | EM / EX / BR | EM / EX / BR | EM / EX / BR | EM / EX / BR |
| | EM / EX / BR | EM / EX / BR | EM / EX / BR | EM / EX / BR | EM / EX / BR |
| | EM / EX / BR | EM / EX / BR | EM / EX / BR | EM / EX / BR | EM / EX / BR |
| | EM / EX / BR | EM / EX / BR | EM / EX / BR | EM / EX / BR | EM / EX / BR |
| | EM / EX / BR | EM / EX / BR | EM / EX / BR | EM / EX / BR | EM / EX / BR |
| | EM / EX / BR | EM / EX / BR | EM / EX / BR | EM / EX / BR | EM / EX / BR |
| | EM / EX / BR | EM / EX / BR | EM / EX / BR | EM / EX / BR | EM / EX / BR |
| | EM / EX / BR | EM / EX / BR | EM / EX / BR | EM / EX / BR | EM / EX / BR |
| | EM / EX / BR | EM / EX / BR | EM / EX / BR | EM / EX / BR | EM / EX / BR |
| | EM / EX / BR | EM / EX / BR | EM / EX / BR | EM / EX / BR | EM / EX / BR |
| | EM / EX / BR | EM / EX / BR | EM / EX / BR | EM / EX / BR | EM / EX / BR |
| | EM / EX / BR | EM / EX / BR | EM / EX / BR | EM / EX / BR | EM / EX / BR |
| | EM / EX / BR | EM / EX / BR | EM / EX / BR | EM / EX / BR | EM / EX / BR |
| | EM / EX / BR | EM / EX / BR | EM / EX / BR | EM / EX / BR | EM / EX / BR |
| | EM / EX / BR | EM / EX / BR | EM / EX / BR | EM / EX / BR | EM / EX / BR |
| | EM / EX / BR | EM / EX / BR | EM / EX / BR | EM / EX / BR | EM / EX / BR |
| | EM / EX / BR | EM / EX / BR | EM / EX / BR | EM / EX / BR | EM / EX / BR |
| | EM / EX / BR | EM / EX / BR | EM / EX / BR | EM / EX / BR | EM / EX / BR |
| | EM / EX / BR | EM / EX / BR | EM / EX / BR | EM / EX / BR | EM / EX / BR |
| | EM / EX / BR | EM / EX / BR | EM / EX / BR | EM / EX / BR | EM / EX / BR |

# ELD Standards Record Sheet

**Teacher:** _____ **Class:** _____

**Standards**: *PII.B.5*

**Guided Activities and Proficiency Levels:**

| Students: | #1 | #2 | #3 | #4 | #5 |
|---|---|---|---|---|---|
| | EM / EX / BR | EM / EX / BR | EM / EX / BR | EM / EX / BR | EM / EX / BR |
| | EM / EX / BR | EM / EX / BR | EM / EX / BR | EM / EX / BR | EM / EX / BR |
| | EM / EX / BR | EM / EX / BR | EM / EX / BR | EM / EX / BR | EM / EX / BR |
| | EM / EX / BR | EM / EX / BR | EM / EX / BR | EM / EX / BR | EM / EX / BR |
| | EM / EX / BR | EM / EX / BR | EM / EX / BR | EM / EX / BR | EM / EX / BR |
| | EM / EX / BR | EM / EX / BR | EM / EX / BR | EM / EX / BR | EM / EX / BR |
| | EM / EX / BR | EM / EX / BR | EM / EX / BR | EM / EX / BR | EM / EX / BR |
| | EM / EX / BR | EM / EX / BR | EM / EX / BR | EM / EX / BR | EM / EX / BR |
| | EM / EX / BR | EM / EX / BR | EM / EX / BR | EM / EX / BR | EM / EX / BR |
| | EM / EX / BR | EM / EX / BR | EM / EX / BR | EM / EX / BR | EM / EX / BR |
| | EM / EX / BR | EM / EX / BR | EM / EX / BR | EM / EX / BR | EM / EX / BR |
| | EM / EX / BR | EM / EX / BR | EM / EX / BR | EM / EX / BR | EM / EX / BR |
| | EM / EX / BR | EM / EX / BR | EM / EX / BR | EM / EX / BR | EM / EX / BR |
| | EM / EX / BR | EM / EX / BR | EM / EX / BR | EM / EX / BR | EM / EX / BR |
| | EM / EX / BR | EM / EX / BR | EM / EX / BR | EM / EX / BR | EM / EX / BR |
| | EM / EX / BR | EM / EX / BR | EM / EX / BR | EM / EX / BR | EM / EX / BR |
| | EM / EX / BR | EM / EX / BR | EM / EX / BR | EM / EX / BR | EM / EX / BR |
| | EM / EX / BR | EM / EX / BR | EM / EX / BR | EM / EX / BR | EM / EX / BR |
| | EM / EX / BR | EM / EX / BR | EM / EX / BR | EM / EX / BR | EM / EX / BR |
| | EM / EX / BR | EM / EX / BR | EM / EX / BR | EM / EX / BR | EM / EX / BR |

**Speaking:** *Retell a Narrative*

# ELD Standards Record Sheet

**Teacher:** _____  **Class:** _____

**Standards:** *PII.C.6*

**Guided Activities and Proficiency Levels:**

| Students: | #1 | #2 | #3 | #4 | #5 |
|---|---|---|---|---|---|
| | EM / EX / BR | EM / EX / BR | EM / EX / BR | EM / EX / BR | EM / EX / BR |
| | EM / EX / BR | EM / EX / BR | EM / EX / BR | EM / EX / BR | EM / EX / BR |
| | EM / EX / BR | EM / EX / BR | EM / EX / BR | EM / EX / BR | EM / EX / BR |
| | EM / EX / BR | EM / EX / BR | EM / EX / BR | EM / EX / BR | EM / EX / BR |
| | EM / EX / BR | EM / EX / BR | EM / EX / BR | EM / EX / BR | EM / EX / BR |
| | EM / EX / BR | EM / EX / BR | EM / EX / BR | EM / EX / BR | EM / EX / BR |
| | EM / EX / BR | EM / EX / BR | EM / EX / BR | EM / EX / BR | EM / EX / BR |
| | EM / EX / BR | EM / EX / BR | EM / EX / BR | EM / EX / BR | EM / EX / BR |
| | EM / EX / BR | EM / EX / BR | EM / EX / BR | EM / EX / BR | EM / EX / BR |
| | EM / EX / BR | EM / EX / BR | EM / EX / BR | EM / EX / BR | EM / EX / BR |
| | EM / EX / BR | EM / EX / BR | EM / EX / BR | EM / EX / BR | EM / EX / BR |
| | EM / EX / BR | EM / EX / BR | EM / EX / BR | EM / EX / BR | EM / EX / BR |
| | EM / EX / BR | EM / EX / BR | EM / EX / BR | EM / EX / BR | EM / EX / BR |
| | EM / EX / BR | EM / EX / BR | EM / EX / BR | EM / EX / BR | EM / EX / BR |
| | EM / EX / BR | EM / EX / BR | EM / EX / BR | EM / EX / BR | EM / EX / BR |
| | EM / EX / BR | EM / EX / BR | EM / EX / BR | EM / EX / BR | EM / EX / BR |
| | EM / EX / BR | EM / EX / BR | EM / EX / BR | EM / EX / BR | EM / EX / BR |
| | EM / EX / BR | EM / EX / BR | EM / EX / BR | EM / EX / BR | EM / EX / BR |
| | EM / EX / BR | EM / EX / BR | EM / EX / BR | EM / EX / BR | EM / EX / BR |
| | EM / EX / BR | EM / EX / BR | EM / EX / BR | EM / EX / BR | EM / EX / BR |

# Practice Activities

---

It is crucial to guide students in having **Constructive Conversations** utilizing skills and strategies that help them develop into productive thinkers and speakers.

- Help students **formulate** their ideas and thinking.
- Help students **explain and extend** their thinking so that it's clear and concise.
- Help students **support** their ideas and thinking with relevant support and information (i.e. from the picture).
- Help students **engage** in constructive dialogue with others through understanding, listening, and **consensus**.

---

**Practice Activities Direction:**

1. Students can work with partners, small group, or with an adult.

2. Students read the story aloud.

3. Students then complete the story map for the following elements: **Characters**, **Setting**, **Beginning**, **Middle**, and **End.**

4. Students then use the sentence starters, sequence words, and the story map to help them retell the story to themselves, a partner, and/or a small group.

# Practice Activity #1

**Directions:** Practice reading the story and retelling the story:

☐ With a partner ☐ In a small group ☐ With an adult

It was Crystal's mom's birthday soon. Crystal decided to make a birthday card for her mom. So she gathered some paper and art supplies from her room.

Crystal started by folding the paper into a card. She then decorated the front of the card with a picture and the words "Happy Birthday!" in big letters.

Next, she wrote a little note on the inside for her mom. She made sure to thank her mom for being such a great mother.

Crystal was excited to give her mom the birthday card. Her mom read the card and loved it! She gave Crystal a big hug.

# Practice Activity #1

## Story Map

### Setting
*Where and when does the story take place?*

### Characters
*Who is the story about?*

### Beginning
*What happened FIRST in the story?*

### Middle
*What happened NEXT in the story?*

### End
*What happened LAST in the story?*

104

# Practice Activity #1

## Retell the Story!

The story is about...

The story takes place...

**First, ...**

**Next, ...**

**Then ...**

**Finally, ...**

# Practice Activity #2

**Directions:** Practice reading the story and retelling the story:

☐ With a partner    ☐ In a small group    ☐ With an adult

Every winter, Sue and her family would hop into the car and drive to the mountains. It was a family tradition to go play in the snow.

Once there, Sue put on her hat, gloves, and scarf. It kept her warm from the frigid cold. She made a huge snowball.

She built a big snowman. She put a big hat on its head. A carrot was used for its nose.

Then Sue and her family had a huge snowball fight. It was fun playing in the snow!

# Practice Activity #2

## Story Map

### Setting
*Where and when does the story take place?*

### Characters
*Who is the story about?*

### Beginning
*What happened FIRST in the story?*

### Middle
*What happened NEXT in the story?*

### End
*What happened LAST in the story?*

# Practice Activity #2

## Retell the Story!

The story is about...

The story takes place...

**First, ...**

**Next, ...**

**Then ...**

**Finally, ...**

# Practice Activity #3

**Directions:** Practice reading the story and retelling the story:

☐ With a partner    ☐ In a small group    ☐ With an adult

Patrick wanted to build a toy race car. He asked his dad for some help. So Patrick and his dad went to the garage to gather some wood and tools.

Patrick's dad helped him glue some pieces of wood together. Then they carved out a car shape and attached some wheels.

Once the car was assembled, Patrick and his dad painted the toy race car a bright red with yellow stripes. It looked awesome!

They took the toy race car outside and tested it out. It glided smoothly and went pretty far. Patrick felt happy.

# Practice Activity #3

## Story Map

### Setting
*Where and when does the story take place?*

### Characters
*Who is the story about?*

### Beginning
*What happened FIRST in the story?*

### Middle
*What happened NEXT in the story?*

### End
*What happened LAST in the story?*

# Practice Activity #3

## Retell the Story!

The story is about...

The story takes place...

**First, ...**

**Next, ...**

**Then ...**

**Finally, ...**

# Practice Activity #4

**Directions:** Practice reading the story and retelling the story:

☐ With a partner ☐ In a small group ☐ With an adult

Victor was conducting an experiment in his class. He wanted to test to see if gravity would affect how fast a ball and a feather will fall.

He wrote down his prediction in his science journal. He predicted that the feather would not fall as fast as the ball.

Victor then stood on a chair. He held the ball and feather out at the same height. He then released the two objects.

Victor concluded that his prediction was right. The ball hit the ground first, while the feather slowly drifted down. Gravity pulled both objects down, but at different rates.

# Practice Activity #4

## Story Map

### Setting
*Where and when does the story take place?*

### Characters
*Who is the story about?*

### Beginning
*What happened FIRST in the story?*

### Middle
*What happened NEXT in the story?*

### End
*What happened LAST in the story?*

# Practice Activity #4

## Retell the Story!

The story is about...

The story takes place...

**First, ...**

**Next, ...**

**Then ...**

**Finally, ...**

# Practice Activity #5

**Directions:** Practice reading the story and retelling the story:

☐ With a partner     ☐ In a small group     ☐ With an adult

Jill had been learning about gardening and vegetables in school. So when she arrived home, she asked her mom if they could plant some vegetables.

Jill's mom took Jill to the store to buy some seeds. In their backyard, Jill planted the seeds into the garden soil. She carefully covered them with the dirt.

Day after day, Jill would go into the backyard garden to water her vegetables. She was excited to see them starting to sprout and grow.

After a few months, Jill and her mom went to check on the garden. The vegetables had grown really big! Jill was excited that she had grown her own vegetables!

# Practice Activity #5

## Story Map

### Setting
*Where and when does the story take place?*

### End
*What happened LAST in the story?*

### Characters
*Who is the story about?*

### Middle
*What happened NEXT in the story?*

### Beginning
*What happened FIRST in the story?*

# Practice Activity #5

## Retell the Story!

The story is about...

The story takes place...

**First, ...**

**Next, ...**

**Then ...**

**Finally, ...**

# Speaking
## *Summarize an Academic Presentation*

**This section includes:**
- Guided Activities
- Teacher's ELD Standards Record Sheet
- Student Practice Activities:
  - Constructive Conversations Guide
  - Summarizing Student Practice

------------------------------------------------

| Alignment to CA ELD Standards: | Alignment to CCSS: |
|---|---|
| **Part I: Interacting in Meaningful Ways** <br> B.5 Listening Actively <br> Listening actively to spoken English in a range of social and academic contexts | SL.3.1–3; L.3.3 <br> SL.4.1–3; L.4.3 <br> SL.5.1–3; L.5.3 |
| **Part I: Interacting in Meaningful Ways** <br> C.9 Presenting <br> Expressing information and ideas in formal oral presentations on academic topics | SL.3.4–6; L.3.1, 3, 6 <br> SL.4.4–6; L.4.1, 3, 6 <br> SL.5.4–6; L.5.1, 3, 6 |
| **Part II: Learning About How English Works** <br> A.2 Structuring Cohesive Texts <br> Understanding Cohesion | RL.3.5; RI.3.5; W.3.1–4; SL.3.4; L.3.1, 3 <br> RL.4.5; RI.4.5; W.4.1–4; SL.4.4; L.4.1, 3 <br> RL.5.5; RI.5.5; W.5.1–4; SL.5.4; L.5.1, 3 |
| **Part II: Learning About How English Works** <br> B.3 Expanding & Enriching Ideas <br> Using verbs and verb phrases | W.3.5; SL.3.6; L.3.1, 3, 6 <br> W.4.5; SL.4.6; L.4.1, 3, 6 <br> W.5.5; SL.5.6; L.5.1, 3, 6 |
| **Part II: Learning About How English Works** <br> B.4 Expanding & Enriching Ideas <br> Using nouns and noun phrases | W.3.5; SL.3.6; L.3.1, 3, 6 <br> W.4.5; SL.4.6; L.4.1, 3, 6 <br> W.5.5; SL.5.6; L.5.1, 3, 6 |
| **Part II: Learning About How English Works** <br> B.5 Expanding & Enriching Ideas <br> Modifying to add details | W.3.5; SL.3.4, 6; L.3.1, 3, 6 <br> W.4.5; SL.4.4, 6; L.4.1, 3, 6 <br> W.5.5; SL.5.4, 6; L.5.1, 3, 6 |

------------------------------------------------

# Speaking
## *Summarize an Academic Presentation*

- - - - - - - - - - - - - - - - - - - - - - - - - - - - - - - - - -

**Alignment to CA ELD Standards:**

**Alignment to CCSS:**

**Part II: Learning About How English Works**
C.6 Expanding & Enriching Ideas
Connecting Ideas

W.3.1-3, 5; SL.3.4, 6; L.3.1, 3, 6
W.4.1–3, 5; SL.4.4, 6; L.4.1, 3, 6
W.5.1–3, 5; SL.5.4, 6; L.5.1, 3, 6

**Part II: Learning About How English Works**
C.7 Expanding & Enriching Ideas
Condensing Ideas

W.3.1-3, 5; SL.3.4, 6; L.3.1, 3, 6
W.4.1–3, 5; SL.4.4, 6; L.4.1, 3, 6
W.5.1–3, 5; SL.5.4, 6; L.5.1, 3, 6

- - - - - - - - - - - - - - - - - - - - - - - - - - - - - - - - - -

**Guided Activities Direction:**
1. Show students the pictures for the academic presentation.
2. Follow the teacher directions.
3. **Say** the **Teacher Script** (indicated by **SAY** ) Read the script similar to how students would hear it as an audio recording on the actual assessment.
4. Guide students through:
   ○ Actively listening to the information
   ○ Taking notes of pertinent information
   ○ Responding with a clear and detailed summary of the academic presentation as supported by the picture
   ○ Providing cohesive and connected ideas
   ○ Include the main points of the academic presentation
   ○ Responding in English with minimal grammatical errors
5. Then have students practice with additional summarizing activities.

# Guided Activity #1

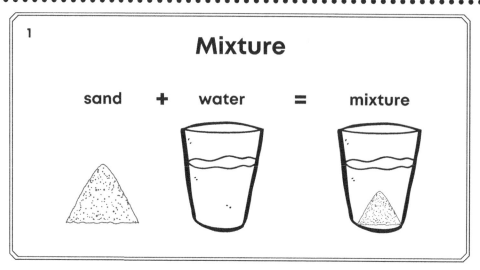

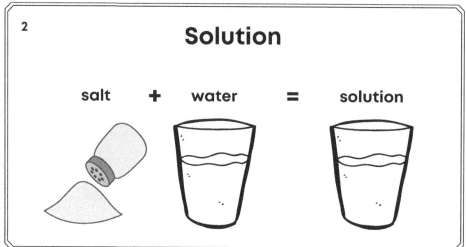

**Speaking:** *Summarize an Academic Presentation*

# Guided Activity #1

 SAY Show the student the pictures.

**You are going to listen to some information about mixtures and solutions.**
**Listen carefully because you will only hear the information ONCE.**
**As you listen, look at the pictures and you may take notes as you listen.**
**When I am finished, you will summarize the information you heard. You**
**will explain the information and use relevant details and clear language.**

SAY

**Have you ever wondered what is the difference between a mixture and a**
**solution? Today we are going to discuss how mixtures and solutions are**
**what is created when you combine various substances together.**

 SAY Point to the corresponding picture as you read the information.

**A mixture is not the same throughout. In other words, a mixture is when**
**two or more substances are combined, but no chemical reaction occurs.**
**Each substance added still maintains its individual properties. An**
**example of a mixture is when sand is added to water. You can still**
**clearly see the sand and water just by looking at it. Each substance did**
**not chemically react with each other and keeps its property.**

 SAY Point to the corresponding picture as you read the information.

**On the other hand, a solution is the same throughout. In other words, a**
**solution is when you combine two or more substances and can no longer**
**see the different properties. A solution is considered homogeneous**
**when the substance is distributed evenly throughout the solution. A**
**great example of a solution is when salt, which is considered the solute,**
**is combined with water, which is the solvent. The sugar dissolves in the**
**water and is no longer visible in it's original form.**

SAY Point to the corresponding picture as you read the information.

**You deal with mixtures and solutions everyday without even realizing it.**
**For instance, when you pour your morning cereal into a bowl of milk, that**
**is a mixture. The cereal and milk maintains its individual properties. On**
**the other hand, when your parents add sugar to their morning coffee**
**then they just created a solution. Mixtures and solutions are simple**
**ways to learn more about chemistry.**

 SAY

**Now it is your turn. Summarize the information you heard. Be sure use**
**relevant details and clear language. Use the pictures to help you.**

# Guided Activity #2

**1** **Atoms**

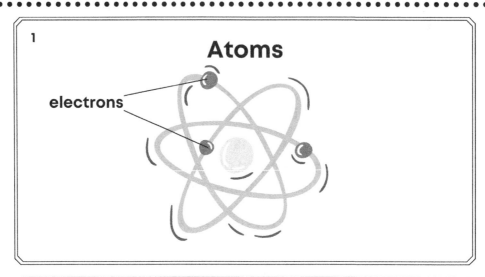

electrons

**2** **Conductors**

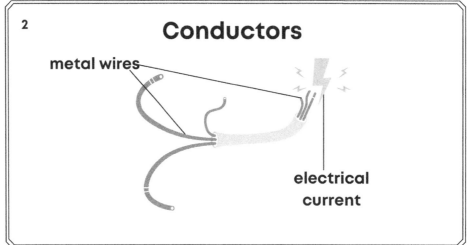

metal wires

electrical current

**3** **Insulators**

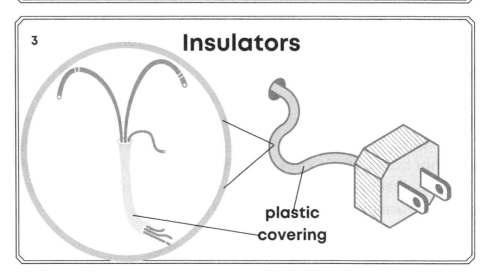

plastic covering

# Guided Activity #2

 **SAY** Show the student the pictures.

**You are going to listen to some information about electrical conductors. Listen carefully because you will only hear the information ONCE. As you listen, look at the pictures and you may take notes as you listen. When I am finished, you will summarize the information you heard. You will explain the information and use relevant details and clear language.**

 **SAY**

**Have you ever wondered how electricity travels from the wall to whatever you just plugged in? Today we are going to discuss electrical conductors, which are materials that allow electricity to flow through.**

 **SAY** Point to the corresponding picture as you read the information.

**A conductor is a material that allows electricity to flow through. What makes a conductor effective has something to do with atoms. Atoms are the basic units of a chemical element. Metals like iron and copper are chemical elements. Atoms have electrons on the outside. An effective conductor has electrons that are loosely bound to the atom and, therefore, can be freely moved when an electric charge is applied.**

 **SAY** Point to the corresponding picture as you read the information.

**In general, some of the best electrical conductors are metals, such as iron and copper. Metals tend to have electrons on the outer layer of their atoms, which makes it easier for electrons to move through the material and carry the electrical current. Many electrical appliances and machines have metal wires that conduct electricity. These metal wires let the electrical current flow through.**

 **SAY** Point to the corresponding picture as you read the information.

**Other materials acts as insulators. These materials stop electrical currents from flowing. An example of an effective insulator is plastic. That is why the cords for electrical appliances and machines are wrapped in plastic. This helps to protect you from the electricity flowing through the metal wires inside.**

 **SAY**

**Now it is your turn. Summarize the information you heard. Be sure use relevant details and clear language. Use the pictures to help you.**

# Guided Activity #3

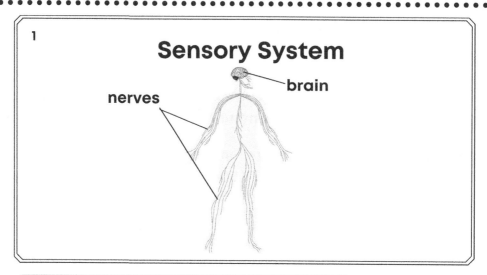

**1** **Sensory System**

brain

nerves

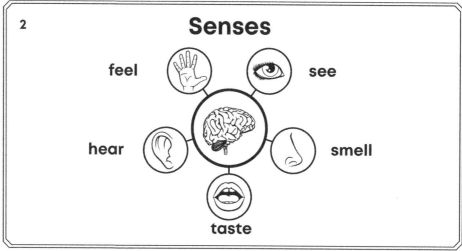

**2** **Senses**

feel · see · hear · smell · taste

**3** **Purpose**

DANGER

smoke (smell)

fire (see, hear, feel)

# Guided Activity #3

 Show the student the pictures.

**You are going to listen to some information about the sensory system. Listen carefully because you will only hear the information ONCE. As you listen, look at the pictures and you may take notes as you listen. When I am finished, you will summarize the information you heard. You will explain the information and use relevant details and clear language.**

 **Do you know why you get chills and goose bumps on your arm when a cold breeze passes by? Today we are going to learn about our sensory system, which is the system that helps us to hear, smell, feel, taste, and see.**

 Point to the corresponding picture as you read the information.

**First of all, our sensory system is made up of a complex network of sensory organs, nerves, and our brain. Our sensory organs takes the information from outside and inside our body and turns it into nerve signals. The signals are then transported rapidly along a network of nerves that connect to the brain. The brain's job is to collect and process all this information quickly.**

 Point to the corresponding picture as you read the information.

**Our sensory system includes the five senses that you are familiar with. You can hear noises and sounds because of the sensitive sensory organs in your ears. You can smell scents and odors because of your nose. You can taste flavors like sour, sweet, bitter, and salty because of the sensory organs in your mouth and on your tongue. Your eyes allows you to see the world around you. Your skin allows you to feel and sense the environment around your body.**

 Point to the corresponding picture as you read the information.

**Your sensory system collects and handles an extraordinary amount of data every second. The purpose of this complex system is to keep you safe, alive, and healthy. For instance, if you get too close to something extremely hot like a fire, your sensory system will warn you and work to get you away from the danger. Your nose can smell smoke and alert you to a fire and have you get to safety.**

 **Now it is your turn. Summarize the information you heard. Be sure use relevant details and clear language. Use the pictures to help you.**

# Guided Activity #4

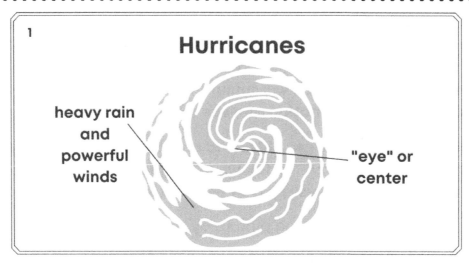

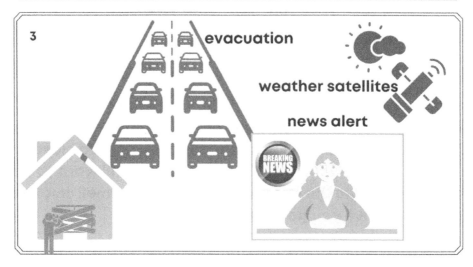

## Speaking: *Summarize an Academic Presentation*

# Guided Activity #4

 **SAY** Show the student the pictures.

**You are going to listen to some information about hurricanes. Listen carefully because you will only hear the information ONCE. As you listen, look at the pictures and you may take notes as you listen. When I am finished, you will summarize the information you heard. You**

 **SAY** **will explain the information and use relevant details and clear language.**

**Have you seen destructive hurricanes that destroy major cities? Today we are going to discuss the cause and effects of a hurricane.**

**SAY** Point to the corresponding picture as you read the information.

**Hurricanes are tropical cyclones that form over the warm waters of the Atlantic Ocean. The term tropical cyclone refers to hurricanes and typhoons. The specific name for the storm depends on where on Earth the storm forms. Hurricanes are circular air movements that start over warm ocean waters near the equator. Strong, powerful winds and heavy rain are driven by humid, warm air rising and rotating. The "eye", or center, of the hurricane is eerily calm with very little wind and rain.**

 **SAY** Point to the corresponding picture as you read the information.

**Hurricanes are classified on a scale of 1 to 5 based on several factors. A category 1 hurricane is considered to be the weakest with wind speeds ranging between 74-95 miles per hour. A category 5 hurricane is the most powerful and destructive with wind speeds reaching over 157 miles per hour. Most recently, Hurricane Ida was a powerful category 4 storm that hit the Gulf Coast of the United States. The destructive hurricane caused major flooding and destroyed buildings and homes and caused billions of dollars in damage. As hurricanes move over land they begin to weaken.**

**SAY** Point to the corresponding picture as you read the information.

**There are many ways people can prepare to stay safe when a hurricane hits. Fortunately, there are many advancements in weather tracking and warning systems that give people ample time to prepare before the hurricane makes landfall. Many people choose to evacuate and leave to safer locations. Other people board up their windows and stock up on emergency supplies and food and water to wait out the storm.**

 **SAY** **Now it is your turn. Summarize the information you heard. Be sure use relevant details and clear language. Use the pictures to help you.**

# Guided Activity #5

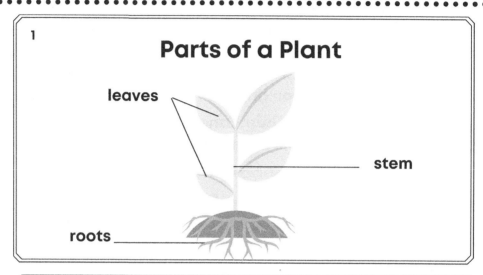

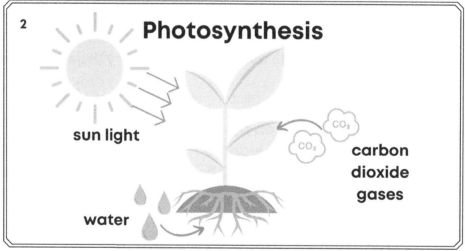

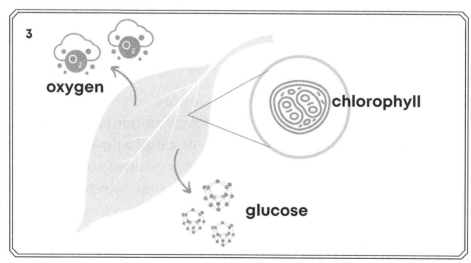

# Guided Activity #5

 Show the student the pictures.

**You are going to listen to some information about photosynthesis. Listen carefully because you will only hear the information ONCE. As you listen, look at the pictures and you may take notes as you listen. When I am finished, you will summarize the information you heard. You will explain the information and use relevant details and clear language.**

 **Have you ever wondered how plants get their nutrients? Today we will discuss photosynthesis which is a process that plants use to make their own food.**

 Point to the corresponding picture as you read the information.

**Photosynthesis is an important biological process by which plants and some microorganisms make their own food. It is a process that requires all parts of the plant. The major parts of the plants are the following: root system, stem, and leaves. The root system absorbs water and nutrients from the soil. The stem helps to transport the water and nutrients to the leaves through a series of inner tubes. The stem also keeps the plant sturdy and upright. The leaves absorb and releases gases from the atmosphere.**

Point to the corresponding picture as you read the information.

**Photosynthesis occurs when the plant's root system absorbs water and nutrients from the soil. The water is then transported up the stems to the plant's leaves. Photosynthesis occurs in the leaves. The leaves contain chlorophyll which are the green pigments that absorb light energy from the sun and carbon dioxide gases from the air.**

 Point to the corresponding picture as you read the information.

**During photosynthesis, the plant utilizes the absorbed sun light, carbon dioxide gases, and water to produce oxygen and glucose. Glucose is a form of sugar that the plants use for growth and development. Photosynthesis benefits the planet and humans because the plant releases the oxygen into the air. In other words, plants and humans need photosynthesis to occur for survival.**

 **Now it is your turn. Summarize the information you heard. Be sure use relevant details and clear language. Use the pictures to help you.**

**Speaking:** *Summarize an Academic Presentation*

# ELD Standards Record Sheet

Directions:

1. Look at the CA ELD standards (**BELOW**) that correspond to this section.
2. Reference these specific standards for the template Record Sheet.
3. Use the following template Record Sheet to monitor students' proficiency levels for the **GUIDED ACTIVITIES** in this section.
4. Fill out all the information. Circle, check, highlight the proficiency level. (*There is space for 20 students. Make additional copies, as needed*)
5. Retain for your records to be used during grading, parent/student conferences, lesson planning, ELD documentation, etc.

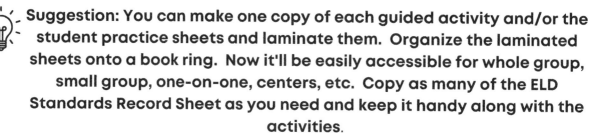 **Suggestion: You can make one copy of each guided activity and/or the student practice sheets and laminate them. Organize the laminated sheets onto a book ring. Now it'll be easily accessible for whole group, small group, one-on-one, centers, etc. Copy as many of the ELD Standards Record Sheet as you need and keep it handy along with the activities.**

# ELD Standards Record Sheet

## CA ELD Standards & Proficiency Levels

**Part I:** Interacting in Meaningful Ways
### B.5 Listening Actively

| EMERGING (EM) | EXPANDING (EX) | BRIDGING (BR) |
|---|---|---|
| Requires **Substantial** Support | Requires **Moderate** Support | Requires **Light** Support |
| **GRADE 3** | | |
| • Demonstrates active listening to:<br> ◦ Read-alouds<br> ◦ Oral presentations<br>• Ask/answer basic questions<br>• Uses support of oral sentence frames<br>• Requires substantial prompting and support | • Demonstrates active listening to:<br> ◦ Read-alouds<br> ◦ Oral presentations<br>• Ask/answer _detailed_ questions<br>• Uses support of oral sentence frames<br>• Requires _occasional_ prompting and moderate support | • Demonstrates active listening to:<br> ◦ Read-alouds<br> ◦ Oral presentations<br>• Ask/answer detailed questions<br>• Requires _minimal_ prompting and light support |
| **GRADE 4** | | |
| • Demonstrates active listening to:<br> ◦ Read-alouds<br> ◦ Oral presentations<br>• Ask/answer basic questions<br>• Requires substantial prompting and support | • Demonstrates active listening to:<br> ◦ Read-alouds<br> ◦ Oral presentations<br>• Ask/answer _detailed_ questions<br>• Requires _occasional_ prompting and moderate support | • Demonstrates active listening to:<br> ◦ Read-alouds<br> ◦ Oral presentations<br>• Ask/answer detailed questions<br>• Requires _minimal_ prompting and light support |
| **GRADE 5** | | |
| • Demonstrates active listening to:<br> ◦ Read-alouds<br> ◦ Oral presentations<br>• Ask/answer basic questions<br>• Requires substantial prompting and support | • Demonstrates active listening to:<br> ◦ Read-alouds<br> ◦ Oral presentations<br>• Ask/answer _detailed_ questions<br>• Requires _occasional_ prompting and moderate support | • Demonstrates active listening to:<br> ◦ Read-alouds<br> ◦ Oral presentations<br>• Ask/answer detailed questions<br>• Requires _minimal_ prompting and light support |

# ELD Standards Record Sheet

## CA ELD Standards & Proficiency Levels:
### Part I: Interacting in Meaningful Ways
### *C.9 Presenting*

| EMERGING (EM) | EXPANDING (EX) | BRIDGING (BR) |
|---|---|---|
| Requires **Substantial** Support | Requires **Moderate** Support | Requires **Light** Support |
| **GRADE 3** | | |
| • *Plan and deliver very brief oral presentations (e.g. retelling a story, describing an animal)*<br>• *Produce basic statements to communicate basic information* | • *Plan and deliver <u>brief</u> oral presentations on a <u>variety of topics</u> (e.g. retelling a story, explaining a science process, etc.)* | • *Plan and deliver <u>longer</u> oral presentations on a variety of topics in a <u>variety of content areas</u> (e.g. retelling a story, explaining a science process or historical event, etc.)* |
| **GRADE 4** | | |
| • *Plan and deliver brief oral presentations on a variety of topics in a variety of content areas: (e.g. retelling a story, explaining a science process, reporting on a current event, recounting a memorable experience, etc.)*<br>• *Requires substantial support* | • *Plan and deliver <u>longer</u> oral presentations on a variety of topics and content areas: (e.g. retelling a story, explaining a science process, reporting on a current event, recounting a memorable experience, etc.)*<br>• *Requires <u>moderate</u> support* | • *Plan and deliver oral presentations on a variety of topics in a variety of content areas:(e.g. retelling a story, explaining a science process, reporting on a current event, recounting a memorable experience, etc.)*<br>• *Requires <u>light</u> support* |
| **GRADE 5** | | |
| • *Plan and deliver brief oral presentations on a variety of topics and content areas: (e.g. providing a report on a current event, reciting a poem, recounting an experience, explaining a science process)*<br>• *Requires moderate support (e.g. graphic organizers)* | • *Plan and deliver <u>longer</u> oral presentations on a variety of topics and content areas: (e.g. providing an opinion speech on a current event, reciting a poem, recounting an experience, explaining a science process)*<br>• *Requires <u>moderate</u> support* | • *Plan and deliver oral presentations on a variety of topics in a variety of content areas: (e.g. providing an opinion speech on a current event, reciting a poem, recounting an experience, explaining a science process)*<br>• *Requires <u>light</u> support* |

# ELD Standards Record Sheet
## CA ELD Standards & Proficiency Levels
**Part II:** Learning About How English Works
### A.2 Understanding Cohesion

| EMERGING (EM) ➤ | EXPANDING (EX) ➤ | BRIDGING (BR) ➤ |
|---|---|---|
| Requires **Substantial** Support | Requires **Moderate** Support | Requires **Light** Support |
| | **GRADE 3** | • Apply *increasing* understanding of language resources that refer the reader back or forward in text<br>• (e.g. how pronouns or synonyms refer back to nouns in text)<br>• Apply *increasing* understanding of how ideas, events, or reasons are linked throughout a text using an *increasing* variety of connecting and *transitional words* or phrases (e.g. for example, afterward, first/next/last)<br>• Comprehend & write cohesive texts |
| • Apply basic understanding of language resources that refer the reader back or forward in text (e.g. how pronouns refer back to nouns in text)<br>• Apply basic understanding of how ideas, events, or reasons are linked throughout a text using every day connecting words or phrases (e.g. then, next)<br>• Comprehend & write basic texts | • Apply *growing* understanding of language resources that refer the reader back or forward in text (e.g. how pronouns refer back to nouns in text)<br>• Apply *growing* understanding of how ideas, events, or reasons are linked throughout a text using a *variety of* connecting words or phrases (e.g. at the beginning/end, first/next)<br>• Comprehend & write texts w/ *increasing* cohesion | |
| | **GRADE 4** | • Apply *increasing* understanding of language resources for referring the reader back or forward in text<br>• (e.g. how pronouns, synonyms, or nominalizations refer back to nouns in text)<br>• Apply *increasing* understanding of how ideas, events, or reasons are linked throughout a text using an *increasing* variety of *academic* connecting and *transitional* words or phrases (e.g. for instance, in addition, at the end)<br>• Comprehend & write cohesive texts |
| • Apply basic understanding of language resources that refer the reader back or forward in text<br>• (e.g. how pronouns refer back to nouns in text)<br>• Apply basic understanding of how ideas, events, or reasons are linked throughout a text using every day connecting words or phrases (e.g. first, yesterday)<br>• Comprehend & write basic texts | • Apply *growing* understanding of language resources for referring the reader back or forward in text (e.g. how pronouns or synonyms refer back to nouns in text)<br>• Apply *growing* understanding of how ideas, events, or reasons are linked throughout a text using a *variety* of connecting words or phrases(e.g. since, next, for example)<br>• Comprehend & write texts w/ *increasing* cohesion | |
| | **GRADE 5** | • Apply *increasing* understanding of language resources for referring the reader back or forward in text (e.g. how pronouns, synonyms, or nominalizations refer back to nouns in text)<br>• Apply *increasing* understanding of how ideas, events, or reasons are linked throughout a text using an *increasing* variety of *academic* connecting and *transitional* words or phrases (e.g. consequently, specifically, however)<br>• Comprehend & write cohesive texts |
| • Apply basic understanding of language resources for referring the reader back or forward in text<br>• (e.g. how pronouns refer back to nouns in text)<br>• Apply basic understanding of how ideas, events, or reasons are linked throughout a text using a select set of every day connecting words or phrases (e.g. first/next, at the beginning)<br>• Comprehend & write basic texts | • Apply *growing* understanding of language resources for referring the reader back or forward in text (e.g. how pronouns or synonyms refer back to nouns in text)<br>• Apply *growing* understanding of how ideas, events, or reasons are linked throughout a text using a *variety* of connecting words or phrases (e.g. for example, in the first place, as a result)<br>• Comprehend & write texts w/ *increasing* cohesion | |

# ELD Standards Record Sheet

## CA ELD Standards & Proficiency Levels

**Part II:** Learning About How English Works
### B.3 Using Verbs and Verb Phrases

| EMERGING (EM) → | EXPANDING (EX) → | BRIDGING (BR) → |
|---|---|---|
| Requires **Substantial** Support | Requires **Moderate** Support | Requires **Light** Support |
| **GRADE 3** | **GRADE 3** | **GRADE 3** |
| • Use frequently used verbs<br>• Use different verb types (e.g. doing, saying, being/having, thinking/feeling)<br>• Use different verb tenses (e.g. simple past for recounting an experience)<br>• Appropriate for the text type and discipline to convey time | • Use a <u>growing number</u> of verb types (e.g. doing, saying, being/having, thinking/feeling)<br>• Use a <u>growing number</u> of verb tenses (e.g. simple past for retelling, simple present for a science description)<br>• Appropriate for the text type and discipline to convey time | • Use a <u>variety</u> of verb types (e.g. doing, saying, being/having, thinking/feeling)<br>• Use a <u>variety</u> of verb tenses (e.g. simple present for a science description, simple future to predict)<br>• Appropriate for the text type and discipline to convey time |
| **GRADE 4** | **GRADE 4** | **GRADE 4** |
| • Use various verbs<br>• Use various verb types (e.g. doing, saying, being/having, thinking/feeling)<br>• Use various verb tenses (e.g. simple past for recounting an experience)<br>• Appropriate for the text type and discipline for familiar topics | • Use various verbs<br>• Use various verb types (e.g. doing, saying, being/having, thinking/feeling)<br>• Use various verb tenses (e.g. simple past for retelling, timeless present for science explanation)<br>• Appropriate for the <u>task</u>, text type and discipline<br>• <u>For an increasing variety of familiar and new topics</u> | • Use various verb<br>• Use various verb types (e.g. doing, saying, being/having, thinking/feeling)<br>• Use various verb tenses(e.g. timeless present for science explanation, mixture of past and present for historical information report)<br>• Appropriate for the task and text type<br>• For a <u>variety</u> of familiar and new topics |
| **GRADE 5** | **GRADE 5** | **GRADE 5** |
| • Use frequently used verbs (e.g. take, like, eat)<br>• Use various verb types (e.g. doing, saying, being/having, thinking/feeling)<br>• Use various verb tenses (e.g. simple past for recounting an experience)<br>• Appropriate for the text type and discipline for familiar topics | • Use <u>various</u> verb types (e.g. doing, saying, being/having, thinking/feeling)<br>• Use various verb tenses (e.g. simple past for retelling, timeless present for science a description)<br>• Appropriate for the <u>task</u>, text type and discipline<br>• <u>For an increasing variety of topics</u> | • Use various verb types (e.g. doing, saying, being/having, thinking/feeling)<br>• Use various verb tenses (e.g. timeless present for science description, mixture of past and present for narrative or history explanation)<br>• Appropriate for the task and text type<br>• For a <u>variety</u> of topics |

134

# ELD Standards Record Sheet

## CA ELD Standards & Proficiency Levels

**Part II:** Learning About How English Works
### *B.4 Using Nouns and Noun Phrases*

| EMERGING (EM) ➤ | EXPANDING (EX) ➤ | BRIDGING (BR) |
|---|---|---|
| *Requires **Substantial** Support* | *Requires **Moderate** Support* | *Requires **Light** Support* |
| | **GRADE 3** | |
| • *Expand noun phrases in simple ways in order to enrich:*<br>◦ *The meaning of sentences*<br>◦ *Add details about ideas, people, things, etc. (e.g. adding an adjective to a noun)* | • *Expand noun phrases in a <u>growing number</u> of ways in order to enrich:*<br>◦ *The meaning of sentences*<br>◦ *Add details about ideas, people, things, etc. (e.g. adding comparative/superlative adjectives to nouns)* | • *Expand noun phrases in a <u>variety</u> of ways in order to enrich:*<br>◦ *The meaning of sentences and*<br>◦ *Add details about ideas, people, things, etc. (e.g. adding comparative/superlative adjectives to nouns, simple clause embedding)* |
| | **GRADE 4** | |
| • *Expand noun phrases in simple ways in order to enrich:*<br>◦ *The meaning of sentences*<br>◦ *Add details about ideas, people, things, etc. (e.g. adding an adjective)* | • *Expand noun phrases in a <u>variety</u> of ways in order to enrich:*<br>◦ *The meaning of sentences*<br>◦ *Add details about ideas, people, things, etc. (e.g. adding adjectives to noun phrases or simple clause embedding)* | • *Expand noun phrases in an <u>increasing variety</u> of ways in order to enrich:*<br>◦ *The meaning of sentences and*<br>◦ *Add details about ideas, people, things, etc. (e.g. adding general academic adjectives and adverbs to noun phrases or more complex clause embedding)* |
| | **GRADE 5** | |
| • *Expand noun phrases in simple ways in order to enrich:*<br>◦ *The meaning of sentences*<br>◦ *Add details about ideas, people, things, etc. (e.g. adding an adjective to a noun)* | • *Expand noun phrases in a <u>variety</u> of ways in order to enrich:*<br>◦ *The meaning of sentences*<br>◦ *Add details about ideas, people, things, etc. (e.g. adding comparative/superlative adjectives to noun phrases or simple clause embedding)* | • *Expand noun phrases in an <u>increasing variety</u> of ways in order to enrich:*<br>◦ *The meaning of sentences*<br>◦ *Add details about ideas, people, things, etc. (e.g. adding comparative/superlative and general academic adjectives to noun phrases or more complex clause embedding)* |

135

# ELD Standards Record Sheet

## CA ELD Standards & Proficiency Levels

<u>**Part II:** Learning About How English Works</u>
### *B.5 Modifying to Add Details*

| EMERGING (EM) | EXPANDING (EX) | BRIDGING (BR) |
|---|---|---|
| *Requires **Substantial** Support* | *Requires **Moderate** Support* | *Requires **Light** Support* |
| | **GRADE 3** | |
| • *Expand sentences with adverbials (e.g. adverbs, adverb phrases, prepositional phrases)*<br>• *Use these to provide details about a familiar activity or process (e.g. time, manner, place, cause) (e.g. They walked to the soccer field.)* | • *Expand sentences with adverbials (e.g. adverbs, adverb phrases, prepositional phrases)*<br>• *Use these to provide details about a familiar or <u>new activity</u> or process (e.g. time, manner, place, cause) (e.g. They worked quietly; They ran across the soccer field.)* | • *Expand sentences with adverbials (e.g. adverbs, adverb phrases, prepositional phrases)*<br>• *Use these to provide details about a <u>range</u> of familiar and new activities or processes. (e.g. time, manner, place, cause) (e.g. They worked quietly all night in their room.)* |
| | **GRADE 4** | |
| • *Expand sentences with familiar adverbials (e.g. basic prepositional phrases)*<br>• *Use these to provide details about a familiar activity or process (e.g. time, manner, place, cause) (e.g. They walked to the soccer field.)* | • *Expand sentences with a <u>growing variety</u> of adverbials (e.g. adverbs, prepositional phrases)*<br>• *Use these to provide details about a familiar or <u>new activity</u> or process (e.g. time, manner, place, cause) (e.g. They worked quietly; They ran across the soccer field.)* | • *Expand sentences with a <u>variety</u> of adverbials (e.g. adverbs, adverb phrases, prepositional phrases)*<br>• *Use these to provide details about a <u>variety</u> of familiar and new activities or processes.(e.g. time, manner, place, cause) (e.g. They worked quietly all night in their room.)* |
| | **GRADE 5** | |
| • *Expand and enrich sentences with adverbials (e.g. adverbs, adverb phrases, prepositional phrases)*<br>• *Use these to provide details about a familiar activity or process (e.g. time, manner, place, cause)* | • *Expand and enrich sentences with adverbials (e.g. adverbs, adverb phrases, prepositional phrases)*<br>• *Use these to provide details about a familiar or <u>new activity</u> or process (e.g. time, manner, place, cause)* | • *Expand and enrich sentences with adverbials (e.g. adverbs, adverb phrases, prepositional phrases)*<br>• *Use these to provide details about a <u>variety</u> of familiar and new activities or processes.(e.g. time, manner, place, cause)* |

# ELD Standards Record Sheet
## CA ELD Standards & Proficiency Levels
### Part II: Learning About How English Works
### *C.6 Connecting Ideas*

| EMERGING (EM) | EXPANDING (EX) | BRIDGING (BR) |
|---|---|---|
| *Requires **Substantial** Support* | *Requires **Moderate** Support* | *Requires **Light** Support* |
| | **GRADE 3** | |
| • *Combine clauses in a few basic ways* <br> • *To make connections between and to join ideas (e.g. creating compound sentences using and, but, so)* | • *Combine clauses in an <u>increasing variety</u> of ways (e.g. creating compound and complex sentences)* <br> • *to make connections between and to join ideas, for example:* <br> ◦ *<u>to express cause/effect (e.g. The deer ran because the mountain lion came.)</u>* <br> ◦ *<u>to make a concession (e.g. She studied all night even though she wasn't feeling well.)</u>* | • *Combine clauses in a <u>wide variety</u> of ways (e.g. creating compound and complex sentences)* <br> • *to make connections between and to join ideas, for example:* <br> ◦ *to express cause/effect (e.g. The deer ran because the mountain lion approached them.)* <br> ◦ *to make a concession(e.g. She studied all night even though she wasn't feeling well.)* <br> ◦ *<u>to link two ideas that happen at the same time (e.g. The cubs played while their mother hunted.)</u>* |
| | **GRADE 4** | |
| • *Combine clauses in a few basic ways* <br> • *To make connections between and to join ideas in sentences (e.g. creating compound sentences using coordinate conjunctions, such as and, but, so)* | • *Combine clauses in an <u>increasing variety</u> of ways (e.g. creating complex sentences using familiar subordinate conjunctions)* <br> • *to make connections between and to join ideas in sentences, for example:* <br> ◦ *<u>to express cause/effect (e.g. The deer ran because the mountain lion came.)</u>* <br> ◦ *<u>to make a concession (e.g. She studied all night even though she wasn't feeling well.)</u>* | • *Combine clauses in a <u>wide variety</u> of ways (e.g. creating complex sentences using a variety of subordinate conjunctions)* <br> • *to make connections between and to join ideas, for example:* <br> ◦ *to express cause/effect (e.g. Since the lion was at the waterhole, the deer ran away.)* <br> ◦ *to make a concession* <br> ◦ *<u>to link two ideas that happen at the same time (e.g. The cubs played while their mother hunted.)</u>* |
| | **GRADE 5** | |
| • *Combine clauses in a few basic ways* <br> • *To make connections between and to join ideas* <br> • *To provide evidence to support ideas or opinions (e.g. You must X because X.)(e.g. creating compound sentences using and, but, so)* | • *Combine clauses in an <u>increasing variety</u> of ways (e.g. creating compound and complex sentences)* <br> • *to make connections between and to join ideas, for example:* <br> ◦ *<u>to express cause/effect (e.g. The deer ran because the mountain lion came.)</u>* <br> ◦ *<u>to make a concession(e.g. She studied all night even though she wasn't feeling well.)</u>* <br> • *To provide reasons to support ideas (e.g. X is an extremely good book because X)* | • *Combine clauses in a <u>wide variety</u> of ways (e.g. creating compound and complex sentences)* <br> • *to make connections between and to join ideas, for example:* <br> ◦ *to express cause/effect (e.g. The deer ran because the mountain lion approached them.)* <br> ◦ *to make a concession (e.g. She studied all night even though she wasn't feeling well.)* <br> ◦ *<u>to link two ideas that happen at the same time (e.g. The cubs played while their mother hunted.)</u>* <br> • *To provide reasons to support ideas (e.g The author persuades the reader by X.)* |

# ELD Standards Record Sheet
## CA ELD Standards & Proficiency Levels
### Part II: Learning About How English Works
### C.7 Condensing Ideas

| EMERGING (EM)—————▶ | EXPANDING (EX) ————— ▶ | BRIDGING (BR) |
|---|---|---|
| *Requires **Substantial** Support* | *Requires **Moderate** Support* | *Requires **Light** Support* |
| **GRADE 3** | | |
| • *Condense clauses in simple ways to create precise and detailed sentences (e.g. It's green. It's red. It's green and red.)* | • *Condense clauses in a <u>growing number</u> of ways to create precise and detailed sentences (e.g. through embedded clauses as in, It's a plant. It's found in the rainforest. It's a green and red plant that's found in the tropical rainforest.)* | • *Condense clauses in a <u>variety of ways</u> to create precise and detailed sentences (e.g. through embedded clauses and other condensing, as in, It's a plant. It's green and red. It's found in the tropical rainforest. It's a green and red plant that's found in the tropical rainforest.)* |
| **GRADE 4** | | |
| • *Condense clauses in simple ways to create precise and detailed sentences (e.g through simple embedded clauses as in, The woman is a doctor. She helps children. The woman is a doctor who helps children.)* | • *Condense clauses in an <u>increasing variety of ways</u> to create precise and detailed sentences (e.g. through a growing number of embedded clauses and other condensing as in, The dog ate quickly. The dog choked. The dog ate so quickly that it choked.)* | • *Condense clauses in a <u>variety of ways</u> to create precise and detailed sentences (e.g. through various types of embedded clauses and other ways of condensing, as in, There was a Gold Rush. It began in the 1850s. It brought a lot of people to California. The Gold Rush that began in the 1850s brought a lot of people to California.)* |
| **GRADE 5** | | |
| • *Condense clauses in simple ways to create precise and detailed sentences (e.g through simple embedded clauses as in, The book is on the desk. The book is mine. The book that is on the desk is mine.)* | • *Condense clauses in an <u>increasing variety of ways</u> to create precise and detailed sentences (e.g. through a growing number of types of embedded clauses and other condensing as in, The book is mine. The book is about science. The book is on the desk.  The science book that's on the desk is mine.)* | • *Condense clauses in a <u>variety of ways</u> to create precise and detailed sentences (e.g. through various types of embedded clauses and some nominalizations, as in, They were a very strong army. They had a lot of enemies. They crushed their enemies because they were strong. Their strength helped them crush their numerous enemies.)* |

**Speaking:** *Summarize an Academic Presentation*

# ELD Standards Record Sheet

**Teacher:** _____ **Class:** _____

**Standards:** *PI.B.5*

**Guided Activities and Proficiency Levels:**

| Students: | #1 | #2 | #3 | #4 | #5 |
|---|---|---|---|---|---|
| | EM / EX / BR | EM / EX / BR | EM / EX / BR | EM / EX / BR | EM / EX / BR |
| | EM / EX / BR | EM / EX / BR | EM / EX / BR | EM / EX / BR | EM / EX / BR |
| | EM / EX / BR | EM / EX / BR | EM / EX / BR | EM / EX / BR | EM / EX / BR |
| | EM / EX / BR | EM / EX / BR | EM / EX / BR | EM / EX / BR | EM / EX / BR |
| | EM / EX / BR | EM / EX / BR | EM / EX / BR | EM / EX / BR | EM / EX / BR |
| | EM / EX / BR | EM / EX / BR | EM / EX / BR | EM / EX / BR | EM / EX / BR |
| | EM / EX / BR | EM / EX / BR | EM / EX / BR | EM / EX / BR | EM / EX / BR |
| | EM / EX / BR | EM / EX / BR | EM / EX / BR | EM / EX / BR | EM / EX / BR |
| | EM / EX / BR | EM / EX / BR | EM / EX / BR | EM / EX / BR | EM / EX / BR |
| | EM / EX / BR | EM / EX / BR | EM / EX / BR | EM / EX / BR | EM / EX / BR |
| | EM / EX / BR | EM / EX / BR | EM / EX / BR | EM / EX / BR | EM / EX / BR |
| | EM / EX / BR | EM / EX / BR | EM / EX / BR | EM / EX / BR | EM / EX / BR |
| | EM / EX / BR | EM / EX / BR | EM / EX / BR | EM / EX / BR | EM / EX / BR |
| | EM / EX / BR | EM / EX / BR | EM / EX / BR | EM / EX / BR | EM / EX / BR |
| | EM / EX / BR | EM / EX / BR | EM / EX / BR | EM / EX / BR | EM / EX / BR |
| | EM / EX / BR | EM / EX / BR | EM / EX / BR | EM / EX / BR | EM / EX / BR |
| | EM / EX / BR | EM / EX / BR | EM / EX / BR | EM / EX / BR | EM / EX / BR |
| | EM / EX / BR | EM / EX / BR | EM / EX / BR | EM / EX / BR | EM / EX / BR |
| | EM / EX / BR | EM / EX / BR | EM / EX / BR | EM / EX / BR | EM / EX / BR |

**Speaking:** *Summarize an Academic Presentation*

# ELD Standards Record Sheet

**Teacher:** _____ **Class:** _____

**Standards:** *PI.C.9*                    **Guided Activities and Proficiency Levels:**

| Students: | #1 | #2 | #3 | #4 | #5 |
|---|---|---|---|---|---|
| | EM / EX / BR | EM / EX / BR | EM / EX / BR | EM / EX / BR | EM / EX / BR |
| | EM / EX / BR | EM / EX / BR | EM / EX / BR | EM / EX / BR | EM / EX / BR |
| | EM / EX / BR | EM / EX / BR | EM / EX / BR | EM / EX / BR | EM / EX / BR |
| | EM / EX / BR | EM / EX / BR | EM / EX / BR | EM / EX / BR | EM / EX / BR |
| | EM / EX / BR | EM / EX / BR | EM / EX / BR | EM / EX / BR | EM / EX / BR |
| | EM / EX / BR | EM / EX / BR | EM / EX / BR | EM / EX / BR | EM / EX / BR |
| | EM / EX / BR | EM / EX / BR | EM / EX / BR | EM / EX / BR | EM / EX / BR |
| | EM / EX / BR | EM / EX / BR | EM / EX / BR | EM / EX / BR | EM / EX / BR |
| | EM / EX / BR | EM / EX / BR | EM / EX / BR | EM / EX / BR | EM / EX / BR |
| | EM / EX / BR | EM / EX / BR | EM / EX / BR | EM / EX / BR | EM / EX / BR |
| | EM / EX / BR | EM / EX / BR | EM / EX / BR | EM / EX / BR | EM / EX / BR |
| | EM / EX / BR | EM / EX / BR | EM / EX / BR | EM / EX / BR | EM / EX / BR |
| | EM / EX / BR | EM / EX / BR | EM / EX / BR | EM / EX / BR | EM / EX / BR |
| | EM / EX / BR | EM / EX / BR | EM / EX / BR | EM / EX / BR | EM / EX / BR |
| | EM / EX / BR | EM / EX / BR | EM / EX / BR | EM / EX / BR | EM / EX / BR |
| | EM / EX / BR | EM / EX / BR | EM / EX / BR | EM / EX / BR | EM / EX / BR |
| | EM / EX / BR | EM / EX / BR | EM / EX / BR | EM / EX / BR | EM / EX / BR |
| | EM / EX / BR | EM / EX / BR | EM / EX / BR | EM / EX / BR | EM / EX / BR |
| | EM / EX / BR | EM / EX / BR | EM / EX / BR | EM / EX / BR | EM / EX / BR |
| | EM / EX / BR | EM / EX / BR | EM / EX / BR | EM / EX / BR | EM / EX / BR |

**Speaking:** *Summarize an Academic Presentation*

# ELD Standards Record Sheet

**Teacher:** _____ **Class:** _____

**Standards**: *PII.A.2*          **Guided Activities and Proficiency Levels:**

| Students: | #1 | #2 | #3 | #4 | #5 |
|---|---|---|---|---|---|
| | EM / EX / BR | EM / EX / BR | EM / EX / BR | EM / EX / BR | EM / EX / BR |
| | EM / EX / BR | EM / EX / BR | EM / EX / BR | EM / EX / BR | EM / EX / BR |
| | EM / EX / BR | EM / EX / BR | EM / EX / BR | EM / EX / BR | EM / EX / BR |
| | EM / EX / BR | EM / EX / BR | EM / EX / BR | EM / EX / BR | EM / EX / BR |
| | EM / EX / BR | EM / EX / BR | EM / EX / BR | EM / EX / BR | EM / EX / BR |
| | EM / EX / BR | EM / EX / BR | EM / EX / BR | EM / EX / BR | EM / EX / BR |
| | EM / EX / BR | EM / EX / BR | EM / EX / BR | EM / EX / BR | EM / EX / BR |
| | EM / EX / BR | EM / EX / BR | EM / EX / BR | EM / EX / BR | EM / EX / BR |
| | EM / EX / BR | EM / EX / BR | EM / EX / BR | EM / EX / BR | EM / EX / BR |
| | EM / EX / BR | EM / EX / BR | EM / EX / BR | EM / EX / BR | EM / EX / BR |
| | EM / EX / BR | EM / EX / BR | EM / EX / BR | EM / EX / BR | EM / EX / BR |
| | EM / EX / BR | EM / EX / BR | EM / EX / BR | EM / EX / BR | EM / EX / BR |
| | EM / EX / BR | EM / EX / BR | EM / EX / BR | EM / EX / BR | EM / EX / BR |
| | EM / EX / BR | EM / EX / BR | EM / EX / BR | EM / EX / BR | EM / EX / BR |
| | EM / EX / BR | EM / EX / BR | EM / EX / BR | EM / EX / BR | EM / EX / BR |
| | EM / EX / BR | EM / EX / BR | EM / EX / BR | EM / EX / BR | EM / EX / BR |
| | EM / EX / BR | EM / EX / BR | EM / EX / BR | EM / EX / BR | EM / EX / BR |
| | EM / EX / BR | EM / EX / BR | EM / EX / BR | EM / EX / BR | EM / EX / BR |
| | EM / EX / BR | EM / EX / BR | EM / EX / BR | EM / EX / BR | EM / EX / BR |

**Speaking:** *Summarize an Academic Presentation*

# ELD Standards Record Sheet

**Teacher:** _____ **Class:** _____

**Standards:** *PII.B.3*

**Guided Activities and Proficiency Levels:**

| Students: | #1 | #2 | #3 | #4 | #5 |
|---|---|---|---|---|---|
| | EM / EX / BR | EM / EX / BR | EM / EX / BR | EM / EX / BR | EM / EX / BR |
| | EM / EX / BR | EM / EX / BR | EM / EX / BR | EM / EX / BR | EM / EX / BR |
| | EM / EX / BR | EM / EX / BR | EM / EX / BR | EM / EX / BR | EM / EX / BR |
| | EM / EX / BR | EM / EX / BR | EM / EX / BR | EM / EX / BR | EM / EX / BR |
| | EM / EX / BR | EM / EX / BR | EM / EX / BR | EM / EX / BR | EM / EX / BR |
| | EM / EX / BR | EM / EX / BR | EM / EX / BR | EM / EX / BR | EM / EX / BR |
| | EM / EX / BR | EM / EX / BR | EM / EX / BR | EM / EX / BR | EM / EX / BR |
| | EM / EX / BR | EM / EX / BR | EM / EX / BR | EM / EX / BR | EM / EX / BR |
| | EM / EX / BR | EM / EX / BR | EM / EX / BR | EM / EX / BR | EM / EX / BR |
| | EM / EX / BR | EM / EX / BR | EM / EX / BR | EM / EX / BR | EM / EX / BR |
| | EM / EX / BR | EM / EX / BR | EM / EX / BR | EM / EX / BR | EM / EX / BR |
| | EM / EX / BR | EM / EX / BR | EM / EX / BR | EM / EX / BR | EM / EX / BR |
| | EM / EX / BR | EM / EX / BR | EM / EX / BR | EM / EX / BR | EM / EX / BR |
| | EM / EX / BR | EM / EX / BR | EM / EX / BR | EM / EX / BR | EM / EX / BR |
| | EM / EX / BR | EM / EX / BR | EM / EX / BR | EM / EX / BR | EM / EX / BR |
| | EM / EX / BR | EM / EX / BR | EM / EX / BR | EM / EX / BR | EM / EX / BR |
| | EM / EX / BR | EM / EX / BR | EM / EX / BR | EM / EX / BR | EM / EX / BR |
| | EM / EX / BR | EM / EX / BR | EM / EX / BR | EM / EX / BR | EM / EX / BR |
| | EM / EX / BR | EM / EX / BR | EM / EX / BR | EM / EX / BR | EM / EX / BR |
| | EM / EX / BR | EM / EX / BR | EM / EX / BR | EM / EX / BR | EM / EX / BR |

# ELD Standards Record Sheet

**Teacher:** _____ **Class:** _____

**Standards**: *PII.B.4*

**Guided Activities and Proficiency Levels:**

| Students: | #1 | #2 | #3 | #4 | #5 |
|---|---|---|---|---|---|
| | EM / EX / BR | EM / EX / BR | EM / EX / BR | EM / EX / BR | EM / EX / BR |
| | EM / EX / BR | EM / EX / BR | EM / EX / BR | EM / EX / BR | EM / EX / BR |
| | EM / EX / BR | EM / EX / BR | EM / EX / BR | EM / EX / BR | EM / EX / BR |
| | EM / EX / BR | EM / EX / BR | EM / EX / BR | EM / EX / BR | EM / EX / BR |
| | EM / EX / BR | EM / EX / BR | EM / EX / BR | EM / EX / BR | EM / EX / BR |
| | EM / EX / BR | EM / EX / BR | EM / EX / BR | EM / EX / BR | EM / EX / BR |
| | EM / EX / BR | EM / EX / BR | EM / EX / BR | EM / EX / BR | EM / EX / BR |
| | EM / EX / BR | EM / EX / BR | EM / EX / BR | EM / EX / BR | EM / EX / BR |
| | EM / EX / BR | EM / EX / BR | EM / EX / BR | EM / EX / BR | EM / EX / BR |
| | EM / EX / BR | EM / EX / BR | EM / EX / BR | EM / EX / BR | EM / EX / BR |
| | EM / EX / BR | EM / EX / BR | EM / EX / BR | EM / EX / BR | EM / EX / BR |
| | EM / EX / BR | EM / EX / BR | EM / EX / BR | EM / EX / BR | EM / EX / BR |
| | EM / EX / BR | EM / EX / BR | EM / EX / BR | EM / EX / BR | EM / EX / BR |
| | EM / EX / BR | EM / EX / BR | EM / EX / BR | EM / EX / BR | EM / EX / BR |
| | EM / EX / BR | EM / EX / BR | EM / EX / BR | EM / EX / BR | EM / EX / BR |
| | EM / EX / BR | EM / EX / BR | EM / EX / BR | EM / EX / BR | EM / EX / BR |
| | EM / EX / BR | EM / EX / BR | EM / EX / BR | EM / EX / BR | EM / EX / BR |
| | EM / EX / BR | EM / EX / BR | EM / EX / BR | EM / EX / BR | EM / EX / BR |
| | EM / EX / BR | EM / EX / BR | EM / EX / BR | EM / EX / BR | EM / EX / BR |

**Speaking:** *Summarize an Academic Presentation*

# ELD Standards Record Sheet

**Teacher:** _____ **Class:** _____

**Standards:** *PII.B.5*

**Guided Activities and Proficiency Levels:**

**Students:**

| | #1 | #2 | #3 | #4 | #5 |
|---|---|---|---|---|---|
| | EM / EX / BR | EM / EX / BR | EM / EX / BR | EM / EX / BR | EM / EX / BR |
| | EM / EX / BR | EM / EX / BR | EM / EX / BR | EM / EX / BR | EM / EX / BR |
| | EM / EX / BR | EM / EX / BR | EM / EX / BR | EM / EX / BR | EM / EX / BR |
| | EM / EX / BR | EM / EX / BR | EM / EX / BR | EM / EX / BR | EM / EX / BR |
| | EM / EX / BR | EM / EX / BR | EM / EX / BR | EM / EX / BR | EM / EX / BR |
| | EM / EX / BR | EM / EX / BR | EM / EX / BR | EM / EX / BR | EM / EX / BR |
| | EM / EX / BR | EM / EX / BR | EM / EX / BR | EM / EX / BR | EM / EX / BR |
| | EM / EX / BR | EM / EX / BR | EM / EX / BR | EM / EX / BR | EM / EX / BR |
| | EM / EX / BR | EM / EX / BR | EM / EX / BR | EM / EX / BR | EM / EX / BR |
| | EM / EX / BR | EM / EX / BR | EM / EX / BR | EM / EX / BR | EM / EX / BR |
| | EM / EX / BR | EM / EX / BR | EM / EX / BR | EM / EX / BR | EM / EX / BR |
| | EM / EX / BR | EM / EX / BR | EM / EX / BR | EM / EX / BR | EM / EX / BR |
| | EM / EX / BR | EM / EX / BR | EM / EX / BR | EM / EX / BR | EM / EX / BR |
| | EM / EX / BR | EM / EX / BR | EM / EX / BR | EM / EX / BR | EM / EX / BR |
| | EM / EX / BR | EM / EX / BR | EM / EX / BR | EM / EX / BR | EM / EX / BR |
| | EM / EX / BR | EM / EX / BR | EM / EX / BR | EM / EX / BR | EM / EX / BR |
| | EM / EX / BR | EM / EX / BR | EM / EX / BR | EM / EX / BR | EM / EX / BR |
| | EM / EX / BR | EM / EX / BR | EM / EX / BR | EM / EX / BR | EM / EX / BR |
| | EM / EX / BR | EM / EX / BR | EM / EX / BR | EM / EX / BR | EM / EX / BR |

# ELD Standards Record Sheet

**Teacher:** _____ **Class:** _____

**Standards:** *PII.C.6*

**Guided Activities and Proficiency Levels:**

| Students: | #1 | #2 | #3 | #4 | #5 |
|---|---|---|---|---|---|
| | EM / EX / BR | EM / EX / BR | EM / EX / BR | EM / EX / BR | EM / EX / BR |
| | EM / EX / BR | EM / EX / BR | EM / EX / BR | EM / EX / BR | EM / EX / BR |
| | EM / EX / BR | EM / EX / BR | EM / EX / BR | EM / EX / BR | EM / EX / BR |
| | EM / EX / BR | EM / EX / BR | EM / EX / BR | EM / EX / BR | EM / EX / BR |
| | EM / EX / BR | EM / EX / BR | EM / EX / BR | EM / EX / BR | EM / EX / BR |
| | EM / EX / BR | EM / EX / BR | EM / EX / BR | EM / EX / BR | EM / EX / BR |
| | EM / EX / BR | EM / EX / BR | EM / EX / BR | EM / EX / BR | EM / EX / BR |
| | EM / EX / BR | EM / EX / BR | EM / EX / BR | EM / EX / BR | EM / EX / BR |
| | EM / EX / BR | EM / EX / BR | EM / EX / BR | EM / EX / BR | EM / EX / BR |
| | EM / EX / BR | EM / EX / BR | EM / EX / BR | EM / EX / BR | EM / EX / BR |
| | EM / EX / BR | EM / EX / BR | EM / EX / BR | EM / EX / BR | EM / EX / BR |
| | EM / EX / BR | EM / EX / BR | EM / EX / BR | EM / EX / BR | EM / EX / BR |
| | EM / EX / BR | EM / EX / BR | EM / EX / BR | EM / EX / BR | EM / EX / BR |
| | EM / EX / BR | EM / EX / BR | EM / EX / BR | EM / EX / BR | EM / EX / BR |
| | EM / EX / BR | EM / EX / BR | EM / EX / BR | EM / EX / BR | EM / EX / BR |
| | EM / EX / BR | EM / EX / BR | EM / EX / BR | EM / EX / BR | EM / EX / BR |
| | EM / EX / BR | EM / EX / BR | EM / EX / BR | EM / EX / BR | EM / EX / BR |
| | EM / EX / BR | EM / EX / BR | EM / EX / BR | EM / EX / BR | EM / EX / BR |
| | EM / EX / BR | EM / EX / BR | EM / EX / BR | EM / EX / BR | EM / EX / BR |

# ELD Standards Record Sheet

**Teacher:** _____ **Class:** _____

**Standards**: *PII.C.7*  **Guided Activities and Proficiency Levels:**

| Students: | #1 | #2 | #3 | #4 | #5 |
|---|---|---|---|---|---|
| | EM / EX / BR | EM / EX / BR | EM / EX / BR | EM / EX / BR | EM / EX / BR |
| | EM / EX / BR | EM / EX / BR | EM / EX / BR | EM / EX / BR | EM / EX / BR |
| | EM / EX / BR | EM / EX / BR | EM / EX / BR | EM / EX / BR | EM / EX / BR |
| | EM / EX / BR | EM / EX / BR | EM / EX / BR | EM / EX / BR | EM / EX / BR |
| | EM / EX / BR | EM / EX / BR | EM / EX / BR | EM / EX / BR | EM / EX / BR |
| | EM / EX / BR | EM / EX / BR | EM / EX / BR | EM / EX / BR | EM / EX / BR |
| | EM / EX / BR | EM / EX / BR | EM / EX / BR | EM / EX / BR | EM / EX / BR |
| | EM / EX / BR | EM / EX / BR | EM / EX / BR | EM / EX / BR | EM / EX / BR |
| | EM / EX / BR | EM / EX / BR | EM / EX / BR | EM / EX / BR | EM / EX / BR |
| | EM / EX / BR | EM / EX / BR | EM / EX / BR | EM / EX / BR | EM / EX / BR |
| | EM / EX / BR | EM / EX / BR | EM / EX / BR | EM / EX / BR | EM / EX / BR |
| | EM / EX / BR | EM / EX / BR | EM / EX / BR | EM / EX / BR | EM / EX / BR |
| | EM / EX / BR | EM / EX / BR | EM / EX / BR | EM / EX / BR | EM / EX / BR |
| | EM / EX / BR | EM / EX / BR | EM / EX / BR | EM / EX / BR | EM / EX / BR |
| | EM / EX / BR | EM / EX / BR | EM / EX / BR | EM / EX / BR | EM / EX / BR |
| | EM / EX / BR | EM / EX / BR | EM / EX / BR | EM / EX / BR | EM / EX / BR |
| | EM / EX / BR | EM / EX / BR | EM / EX / BR | EM / EX / BR | EM / EX / BR |
| | EM / EX / BR | EM / EX / BR | EM / EX / BR | EM / EX / BR | EM / EX / BR |
| | EM / EX / BR | EM / EX / BR | EM / EX / BR | EM / EX / BR | EM / EX / BR |
| | EM / EX / BR | EM / EX / BR | EM / EX / BR | EM / EX / BR | EM / EX / BR |

# Practice Activities

------------------------------------------------------------

It is crucial to guide students in having **Constructive Conversations** utilizing skills and strategies that help them develop into productive thinkers and speakers.

- Help students **formulate** their ideas and thinking.
- Help students **explain and extend** their thinking so that it's clear and concise.
- Help students **support** their ideas and thinking with relevant support and information (i.e. from the picture).
- Help students **engage** in constructive dialogue with others through understanding, listening, and **consensus**.

------------------------------------------------------------

**Practice Activities Direction:**

1. Students can work with partners, small group, or with an adult.

2. Students read the academic presentation aloud.

3. Students then complete the summary map for the following elements: **Topic**, **Main Idea**, and **Details**.

4. Students then use the sentence starters, transition words, and the summary map to help them summarize the academic presentation.

# Practice Activity #1

**Directions:** Practice reading the academic presentation:

☐ With a partner    ☐ In a small group    ☐ With an adult

## The Ocean

This is the ocean.  There are seven major oceans in the world.  The oceans cover over 70% of the Earth's surface.  Oceans are large bodies of salt water.  They are both deep and wide and the ocean floor is covered by deep valleys and large mountain ranges.

The ocean is very important.  Many different plants and animals live in the ocean.  In fact, the majority Earth's life can be found in the oceans.  Fish, sharks, whales, and dolphins live in this aquatic environment.  Seaweed is one type of plant in the ocean.

It is vital or important to protect the oceans.  Not only for the sake of the marine life, but also for human survival.  The oceans help to regulate the Earth's temperature.  If the ocean temperatures rises, then the Earth will get warmer.  This climate change is dangerous.

# Practice Activity #1

## Summary Map

### Main Idea
*What is the most important idea?*

### Topic
*What is the presentation about?*

### Detail #3
*One important fact*

### Detail #2
*One important fact*

### Detail #1
*One important fact*

# Practice Activity #1

## Summarize the Academic Presentation
Use the text, story map, and sentence starters below.

*The topic of the presentation is...*

*The main idea is...*

*One important detail is...*
*For example, in the text it says...*

*A second important detail is...*
*An example from the text is...*

*A third important detail is...*
*The support from the text is...*

*In conclusion, ...*

# Practice Activity #2

**Directions:** Practice reading the academic presentation:

☐ With a partner ☐ In a small group ☐ With an adult

## Human Brain

This is the human brain. The brain is a very complex and important organ. It weighs about three pounds and 60% of it is made of fat. It has a soft, jelly-like feel to it. It is protected by our skull, which is a hard bone. However, despite its extremely delicate nature, the human brain is one of the most complex and advanced "computers" out there!

The brain is the control center of our body. It helps us do many things like think, feel, and move. It regulates our breathing, heart rate, body temperature, and practically everything else in our bodies. It has an unlimited storage capacity, which means that our brains can store a lot of information.

There is still a lot that we do not know about our own brains. However, it makes us the smartest animals on Earth!

# Practice Activity #2

## Summary Map

### Main Idea
*What is the most important idea?*

### Topic
*What is the presentation about?*

### Detail #3
*One important fact*

### Detail #2
*One important fact*

### Detail #1
*One important fact*

# Practice Activity #2

## Summarize the Academic Presentation
Use the text, story map, and sentence starters below.

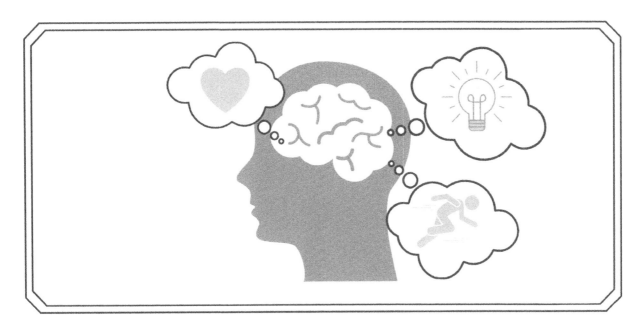

*The topic of the presentation is...*

*The main idea is...*

*One important detail is...*
*For example, in the text it says...*

*A second important detail is...*
*An example from the text is...*

*A third important detail is...*
*The support from the text is...*

*In conclusion, ...*

# Practice Activity #3

**Directions:** Practice reading the academic presentation:

☐ With a partner  ☐ In a small group  ☐ With an adult

## The Grasslands

Grasslands are one of Earth's major biomes or large natural areas. The grasslands are dominated by large, open areas of grass. They can be found on every continent, except for Antarctica. Most people think of Africa when they learn about grasslands.

Many different plants and animals live in the grasslands. Giraffes with long necks eat leaves from the occasional trees. Big elephants roam the vast landscape. Lions hide and hunt among the tall grass. Many animals graze on the abundant grass. The grasslands are full of life.

Humans also depend on the grassland biome. Some grasslands have been converted to farms because the rich soil is ideal for growing crops. However, too much destruction of the grasslands can greatly impact the plants and animals that live there.

# Practice Activity #3

## Summary Map

### Main Idea
*What is the most important idea?*

### Topic
*What is the presentation about?*

### Detail #3
*One important fact*

### Detail #2
*One important fact*

### Detail #1
*One important fact*

# Practice Activity #3

## Summarize the Academic Presentation
Use the text, story map, and sentence starters below.

*The topic of the presentation is...*

*The main idea is...*

*One important detail is...*
*For example, in the text it says...*

*A second important detail is...*
*An example from the text is...*

*A third important detail is...*
*The support from the text is...*

*In conclusion, ...*

# Practice Activity #4

**Directions:** Practice reading the academic presentation:

☐ With a partner    ☐ In a small group    ☐ With an adult

## Pets

Do you have a pet?  Is it a dog or cat?  Or maybe it's a bird!  There are many different types of pets.  Pets are animals that people have as a companion.

The most common type of pets are dogs and cats.  Some people have dogs because they are playful.  Other people have cats because they are a little more subdued and they tend to keep to themselves.  However, both animals bring a lot of love and happiness to their owners.  Birds can be pets also.  They like to chirp and sing.  Some people keep exotic birds like parrots and parakeets as pets.  These color birds can sometimes be taught to talk.

Research has shown that owning a pet helps people live longer and happier lives.  Pets make people happy and they also keep people active and on the go!

# Practice Activity #4

## Summary Map

### Main Idea
*What is the most important idea?*

### Topic
*What is the presentation about?*

### Detail #3
*One important fact*

### Detail #2
*One important fact*

### Detail #1
*One important fact*

# Practice Activity #4

## Summarize the Academic Presentation
Use the text, story map, and sentence starters below.

The topic of the presentation is...

The main idea is...

One important detail is...
For example, in the text it says...

A second important detail is...
An example from the text is...

A third important detail is...
The support from the text is...

In conclusion, ...

# Practice Activity #5

**Directions:** Practice reading the academic presentation:

☐ With a partner  ☐ In a small group  ☐ With an adult

## Life Cycle of a Butterfly

Have you ever observed a delicate, beautiful butterfly fluttering around a flower?  Do you know where that butterfly came from?  This is the life cycle of a butterfly.

It all starts with eggs that are hatched onto a leaf.  When the eggs hatch it slowly develops into a caterpillar.  The caterpillar is a kind of larva or young version of a butterfly.  A caterpillar is an insect that feeds on leaves.

Soon after, the caterpillar then wraps itself into a silk cocoon and becomes a pupa.  It hangs under a leaf while it slowly changes and develops into a butterfly.

After some time, a beautiful butterfly emerges from the pupa.  It dries its wings in the warm sun before fluttering away.

# Practice Activity #5

## Summary Map

### Main Idea
*What is the most important idea?*

### Topic
*What is the presentation about?*

### Detail #1
*One important fact*

### Detail #2
*One important fact*

### Detail #3
*One important fact*

# Practice Activity #5

## Summarize the Academic Presentation

Use the text, story map, and sentence starters below.

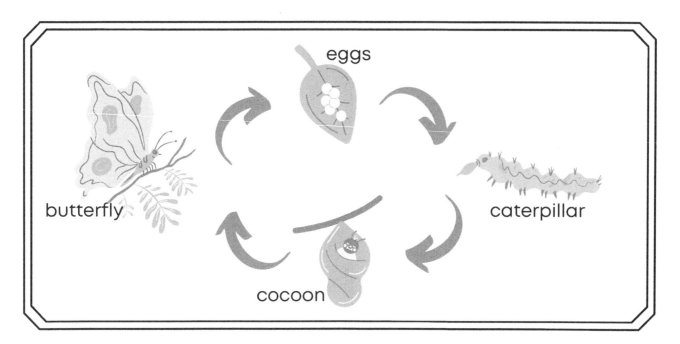

*The topic of the presentation is...*

*The main idea is...*

*One important detail is...*
*For example, in the text it says...*

*A second important detail is...*
*An example from the text is...*

*A third important detail is...*
*The support from the text is...*

*In conclusion, ...*

THIS PAGE INTENTIONALLY LEFT BLANK

Made in United States
Orlando, FL
19 September 2024

51712145R00091